latin d'lite

latin d'lite

delicious latin recipes with a healthy twist

ingrid
hoffmann

A CELEBRA BOOK

CELELBRA
Published by the Penguin Group
Penguin Group (USA) Inc., 375 Hudson Street,
New York, New York 10014, USA
Penguin Group (Canada), 90 Eglinton Avenue East, Suite 700, Toronto,
Ontario M4P 2Y3, Canada (a division of Pearson Penguin Canada Inc.)
Penguin Books Ltd., 80 Strand, London WC2R 0RL, England
Penguin Ireland, 25 St. Stephen's Green, Dublin 2,
Ireland (a division of Penguin Books Ltd.)
Penguin Group (Australia), 707 Collins Street, Melbourne, Victoria 3008,
Australia (a division of Pearson Australia Group Pty. Ltd.)
Penguin Books India Pvt. Ltd., 11 Community Centre, Panchsheel Park,
New Delhi–110 017, India
Penguin Group (NZ), 67 Apollo Drive, Rosedale, Auckland 0632,
New Zealand (a division of Pearson New Zealand Ltd.)
Penguin Books (South Africa), Rosebank Office Park, 181 Jan Smuts Avenue,
Parktown North 2193, South Africa
Penguin China, B7 Jiaming Center, 27 East Third Ring Road North,
Chaoyang District, Beijing 100020, China

Penguin Books Ltd., Registered Offices:
80 Strand, London WC2R 0RL, England

Published by Celebra,
a division of Penguin Group (USA) Inc.

First Printing, April 2013
10 9 8 7 6 5 4 3 2 1

LIBRARY OF CONGRESS CATALOGING-IN-PUBLICATION DATA:
Hoffmann, Ingrid.
Latin D'lite: delicious Latin recipes with a healthy twist/Ingrid Hoffmann.
p. cm.
Includes index.
ISBN 978-0-451-41627-8
1. Cooking, Latin American. 2. Low-fat diet—Recipes.
3. Low-calorie diet—Recipes. I. Title.
TX716.A1H613 2013
641.598—dc23   2012032959

Set in Archer
Designed by Pauline Neuwirth

PUBLISHER'S NOTE
The recipes contained in this book are to be followed exactly as written. The publisher
is not responsible for your specific health or allergy needs that may require medical
supervision. The publisher is not responsible for any adverse reactions to the recipes
contained in this book.
   While the author has made every effort to provide accurate telephone numbers,
Internet addresses and other contact information at the time of publication, neither the
publisher nor the author assumes any responsibility for errors, or for changes that occur
after publication. Further, publisher does not have any control over and does not assume
any responsibility for author or third-party Web sites or their content.

To my father

Papi, I dedicate this book to you because you define all it means to me. Thank you for leading by example and teaching me the importance of a great work ethic and for always telling me to find a job I loved and do it with passion. Thank you for sharing your love of food with me while always highlighting the importance of living a healthy life filled with balance. I love you and will miss you always!

To Delia

You have been the backbone of my business and a trusted friend for many years now and the engine behind me. Thanks for all your hard work, love and dedication to Ingrid Inc. I love you and thank you. You made this book happen!

To all our people in the fields working hard labor for us to eat.

contents

introduction

i've always loved and been obsessed with food. My life—personal and professional—revolves around food. My fondest memories are attached to food and sharing meals with my family and my friends.

Sometimes I have loved food too much and too often. When I tried whatever crazy diet was hot at the moment—low-carb, no-carb, low-fat, no-fat—I always failed because I felt deprived and hungry. I went back to my old ways, and not having control of my food made me feel like a failure.

At some point, I realized that I simply could not keep eating or drinking as I was. The pounds just kept piling onto my hips and waist, and it became harder to get rid of them. When I was diagnosed with an inflammatory disease, I understood why I was always feeling so sluggish and slow. My research and discussions with doctors and nutritional experts showed that much of what I was eating was having a negative effect on my health and well-being. I knew I had to change my cooking and eating habits as well as my thinking about food. I was determined to find a new approach and change my lifestyle rather than go back to dieting and depriving myself. The big question was, Could I do it without giving up the bold and hearty Latin dishes I adore and have been eating all of my life? Did this mean I could still eat rice and beans? The South American beef dishes of my childhood? The paellas and moles of my travels?

The answer is yes!

I was able to improve my health by changing my eating habits, yet stay true to my culinary roots and heritage. *Latin D'lite* is the culmination of this journey and offers more than 150 of my favorite recipes from Latin America and Spain. These dishes are lighter and healthier, yet they are bursting with the same bold flavors found in the traditional preparations.

The secret to my system is making small but significant changes to how I cook and eat. I used to put three tablespoons of sugar in every cup of coffee, but cut back to two, then one, and now I drink it black—without milk or sweetener. Instead of two slices of white toast with butter and jam or cheese for breakfast, I eat scrambled organic egg whites with vegetables or drink a fruit smoothie made with nonfat milk and a scoop of protein powder. I make sure there's at least one vegetable or salad on my plate at every meal. I cook more fish and poultry and less red meat. When I'm craving something starchy, I have

brown rice or quinoa. I use less fat—and no butter—but punch up my cooking with herbs, citrus juices, and different vinegars. I enjoy between-meal treats—like half of an avocado or a piece of fruit—because it's healthful snacking that keeps me from becoming ravenous and overeating when I sit down to a meal. I could never cook without my beloved chiles, spices, tropical fruits, and tubers. Fortunately they are low in calories and fat, so I continue to enjoy the Latin flavors and foods I adore. I taught myself to think about where my food comes from. Did it come out of the ground or out of a can or package? Did it have a mother? I eat closer to nature and stay as far away from processed foods as possible.

My recipes in *Latin D'lite* also allow you the occasional splurge while making these healthy changes and sticking to them. Yes, that's right. Splurge! At the end of each chapter, there's a recipe for an "indulgence." I'm a firm believer that we should be allowed to eat whatever we want in moderation.

Through simple yet effective changes such as substituting healthy ingredients for not so healthy ones and still leaving room for the occasional splurge, I've learned how to maintain my weight, improve my health, and never feel deprived. This lifestyle change has made all the difference in the world for me, and I know my approach can work for you, too.

Remember, if I can do it, you can do it.

With love and gratitude,
Ingrid

introduction

ingredients and healthy substitutions

for me, making lifestyle changes and a commitment to living well means thinking about what ingredients will give me the most flavor and the fewest calories. I discovered that I didn't miss butter, cheese, sugar, and other high-calorie and high-fat foods when I used more herbs, spices, and other seasonings and healthy substitutions. These are the ingredients I always have in my pantry and can't live without.

HERBS, SPICES, AND OTHER SEASONINGS

Food always tastes better when it's well seasoned. I find this to be especially true when cooking without a lot of high-fat ingredients like butter, cream, and other dairy products. Always taste your food as you're cooking to see if it needs another pinch of salt or a measure of some fresh herbs.

herbs

Herbs—the leaves of certain plants—are best when they're fresh. Fresh herbs are available almost everywhere, but if you have to use dried

herbs, crush them with a mortar and pestle or in your hands to release their essential oils. To keep herbs fresh for as long as possible, wrap them in a damp paper towel and place in a plastic bag. Wash them just before using.

Basil perks up salads, dressings, and fish dishes with its slight licorice flavor. Float some

chopped basil leaves on soups and stews. Pair basil with vegetable dishes, especially tomatoes.

Bay leaves release their flavors during cooking. Look for Turkish bay leaves; they're the best. Add just one or two whole bay leaves to soups, stews, and seafood dishes. Be sure to remove the leaves before serving, because they have sharp edges and an unpleasant taste.

Cilantro is the one herb I can't cook without. I use handfuls of it in salsas, soups, and stews. I find picking all the leaves off the stems time-consuming and unnecessary, so I just chop up the stems as well as leaves. Cilantro can be quite sandy, so wash it thoroughly in several changes of water before chopping.

Mint can be used in sweet and savory dishes. Fuzzy spearmint and peppermint are what I use most often, but I also like to try the more exotic varieties, like apple mint and chocolate mint, that are found at farmers' markets. Muddle some mint leaves for cocktails; add it to salsas and salads.

Oregano comes from the Old World—the Mediterranean—as well as the New World—Mexico. Although the different varieties have similar flavor profiles, they come from two different plants. Mexican oregano tends to be stronger and less sweet than its Mediterranean sister. They can be used interchangeably, so don't fret if you can't find Mexican oregano. And if you can't find it fresh, using dried is perfectly acceptable. Whichever kind you use—Mediterranean or Mexican—add the oregano at the beginning of cooking your vegetables, meats, or other ingredients so the herb has time to develop its flavor.

Parsley adds a fresh, bright flavor whether used in cooking or as a garnish. I prefer Italian flat-leaf parsley with its slightly peppery taste; it holds up better in cooking than curly parsley. I often use it in combination with cilantro. Always keep a bunch on hand to use whenever a dish needs a sprinkle of fresh green color and herb-alicious taste.

Rosemary has an intense lemon-pine scent and a flavor that goes well with beans, chicken, pork, and braised dishes. Strip the leaves, or needles, off the stems before adding to your cooking. Be sure to try my Rosemary Syrup (page 281) in cocktails.

Thyme is another Mediterranean herb that's become popular everywhere. Strip the small leaves from the stems and use them in recipes with tomatoes, olives, and onions. Thyme is a great companion to other herbs, so use it in combination with parsley, rosemary, and oregano.

spices

We recognize different culinary traditions by the kinds of spices found in dishes. A chicken dish with saffron and smoked paprika says Spain, but if made with a *bouquet garni* (a bundle of herbs) of bay, thyme, and parsley, it screams French. Latin food is well-known for its generous use of spices. Here are the ones to keep in your pantry—in sealed containers away from light.

Cumin imparts a nutty, peppery boldness to vegetables, grains, fish, and meats. Keep cumin seeds and ground cumin in your pantry.

Saffron gives paella and other dishes a soft yellow-orange hue. Saffron is expensive because the orange threads from the crocus plant are hand harvested. A little bit of top-quality Spanish saffron—it's the best—goes a long way. And buyer beware: Inexpensive turmeric is sometimes sold as a substitute.

Salt comes in many varieties: Kosher salt is the one I put to work more than any other when cooking. Fine-grained table salt has additives to keep it free-flowing, making it ideal for baking. Fine- or coarse-grained sea salt is just that—the salt left behind after seawater has evaporated. Because it has a bright, briny flavor, don't waste costly sea salt on general cooking, like salting the water to boil pasta. Sprinkle it on food as a finishing salt.

Smoked paprika, or *pimentón*, comes from small red peppers that are dried and then smoked in the Murcia or La Vera regions of Spain. Use just a bit to add cooked-over-a-wood-fire smokiness to paella and chicken dishes. There are three types of smoked paprika: *Pimentón dulce* (sweet paprika) has a hint of sweet-ness and is light orange in color; *pimentón agridulce* (medium hot paprika) has a jolt of heat and is darker; and *pimentón picante* (hot paprika) is just what its name says. I keep the first two in my pantry. Once difficult to find except at gourmet shops, *pimentón* can now be found in markets everywhere.

other seasonings

Achiote, also called annatto seed, imparts a rusty red color and a hint of pungency to food. Rather than use the seeds directly, heat about ½ cup in canola or other vegetable oil (1 cup) and strain. It is the oil that is used in cooking chicken, fish, beef, pork or rice. The strained oil will keep in the refrigerator for 1 month. Achiote also comes in paste and powder forms. Wear gloves when handling achiote as it is also used as dye and will stain your hands.

ingredients and healthy substitutions

Adobo seasoning is considered the salt and pepper of Latin food. You just can't cook without it. A spice blend of herbs, chile powder, salt, cumin, and other seasonings, adobo is used in everything from soups to stews to chicken and seafood. While commercial adobo seasoning mixes are available, I find that they're way too salty for my taste, so I make my own Delicioso Adobo Seasoning. Try my recipe, but feel free to double the amounts below or make it your own by adding more or less of each ingredient. The amount below makes a little bit less than 1 cup of seasoning. Your adobo will only be as good as your ingredients; be sure they're fresh.

DELICIOSO ADOBO SEASONING

2 tablespoons lemon pepper

2 tablespoons garlic powder

2 tablespoons onion powder or flakes

2 tablespoons dried oregano

2 tablespoons dried parsley flakes

2 tablespoons achiote powder

1 tablespoon ground cumin

2 tablespoons kosher salt

Combine all of the ingredients in a small glass jar with an airtight lid and shake to blend. Keep in a cool, dark place up to two months.

BEANS AND GRAINS

Rice and **beans** have nourished people for centuries. Together, they make a complete protein, which is essential for the body's growth and de-velopment. My family ate white rice and beans at every meal no matter where we lived when I was growing up. It remains one of my favorite dishes, but I find that just a small serving is plenty. And both are budget friendly; 1 pound of high-protein, high-fiber dried beans will make 14 servings, which you can store and freeze for multiple meals.

Beans come in a rainbow of color and endless varieties—black, red, pinto, fava, lima, white. When I have time, I soak dried beans overnight with a little baking soda to make them easily digestible and cook them the following day. If not, I cook dried beans in my pressure cooker—no soaking required.

Check the date on dried beans and peas to make sure they haven't been sitting on the market shelves for too long! The longer they sit, the longer it will take to cook. And don't discard that delicious bean broth! Use it as a gravy.

My pantry is also packed with canned beans, because nothing beats their convenience when you want a fast, healthful meal. Always rinse and drain canned beans well to get rid of excess salt, unless otherwise noted in a recipe.

While I grew up eating white rice and still do on occasion, I prefer brown rice these days. Brown rice retains more of its nutritional value than white. It does take longer to cook than white rice, but check out my recipe for brown rice quickly made in a pressure cooker (page 234).

Quinoa is an ancient seed that was first grown on both sides of the Andes Mountains in Bolivia and Peru. While quinoa has become more popular in recent years, my family ate it often because it was a staple on the table of my Bolivian grandfather, Eduardo Ybarnegaray, when he was growing up. Packed with essential amino acids and good-for-you minerals, gluten-free quinoa can be used as a substitute for rice or pasta and served hot or cold in salads and soups. Best of all, quinoa cooks in less than five minutes.

SWEETENERS

As I've taught myself to eat fewer processed foods, I've discovered a whole new world of ingredients that can be used as sweeteners. Some recipes require refined white, brown, or confectioners' sugar or honey, which is fine. You don't necessarily need to sacrifice taste for nutritional value. But as I mentioned before, the *Latin D'lite* way is to use these ingredients in moderation.

Stevia, also known as sweet leaf, comes from a South American herb. It's my favorite sweetener because it contains no calories and no carbs and it is available in tablet, liquid, or powdered form. I prefer to use the powder that comes in individual packages. Stevia is, however, intensely sweet, so use just a drop or pinch to start.

Agave nectar is a brown natural sweetener that comes from the same plant as tequila. Since it has no aftertaste or distinct flavor, agave can be used in smoothies, sauces, and other dishes that need a touch of sweetness. Light and dark agave can be used interchangeably. Substitute ⅓ cup agave for every 1 cup sugar.

Coconut, specifically sweetened coconut flakes, can be used in *batidos* and desserts as a sweetener. I also use it to dredge chicken and fish fillets.

Dried fruits and **fruit pastes**: You name a fresh tropical fruit—guava, pineapple, papaya, passion fruit, mango—and chances are they are also available dried, as a fruit paste, or a juice. Look for dried fruit that has been treated without sulfates. They may not look as pretty as the ones with preservatives, but they're better for you. A mango or guava paste or a few tablespoons of fruit nectar add just the right touch of sweetness to desserts and sauces.

NUTS AND SEEDS

Latin cuisine has long used nuts and seeds as ingredients in soups and sauces. Romesco and picada sauces from Spain and moles from the New World are the best known. Make sure the nuts you buy are fresh, because they can quickly turn rancid. I keep mine in the freezer to maintain their shelf life. Toasting nuts and seeds

brings out their true flavors. A handful—just one!—of mixed nuts and seeds is a healthy snack that provides energy and protein to keep you going.

Almonds, **walnuts**, **pine nuts**, and **hazelnuts** are used most frequently in Latin cooking and as a garnish. To toast nuts, spread the nuts in a single layer on a rimmed baking sheet. Bake in a preheated 350°F oven, stirring occasionally, until toasted and fragrant, about 10 minutes. Watch them carefully; they can burn in an instant. Let them cool completely. For hazelnuts, wrap the hot nuts in a clean dish towel. Rub the nuts through the towel to remove the skin. Don't worry if some of the skins remain on the nuts. Cool the nuts before using.

Pumpkin seeds, or *pepitas* in Spanish, are used frequently to thicken and add body to dishes like moles and other sauces. Look for hulled pumpkin seeds and add them to muffin batters or use them as a garnish for salads instead of croutons. You can buy roasted or raw, salted or unsalted. I prefer to buy raw, unsalted *pepitas* and roast and season them myself. Spread the seeds on a parchment paper–lined baking sheet. Bake them in a preheated 350°F oven for 10 to 15 minutes, or until browned.

CHILES

I can't imagine Latin food without our beloved chiles! We use them fresh and dried, canned and pickled, in cooking and as a garnish. If you can't find the chiles listed below, feel free to substitute. I like my food medium hot, but use more or less depending on your personal preference. Most of a chile's heat is in the seeds and veins,

so remove them with a knife if you want a milder flavor. Bottled hot sauce—there are so many brands—is good to keep on hand. Add just a few drops at a time.

Ají amarillo: If a chile could taste like sunshine, then *ají amarillo* would be it! This bright yellow Peruvian pepper starts off sweet and fruity; then a hint of heat kicks in at the end. Essential to Peruvian food, it is one of my favorite chiles. Look for fresh or dry chiles or pastes.

Ají dulce (*dulce* means "sweet"), also known as *ají cachucha*, is a small mild pepper from South America. It looks like a habanero but doesn't have the same level of heat and is often used in a sofrito for just a touch of warmth.

Ají panca: Slightly smoky and mild, *ají panca* chiles have long been grown in Peru. The paste is available in jars online or in some markets, sometimes labeled "Sun-Dried Red-Hot Pepper Paste." Stir a bit into seafood, pork, or other stews. If you can't find it, substitute pasilla chile paste, which is available in many markets.

Chipotle peppers are red jalapeño peppers that have been dried over smoke to bring out their rich flavor. Chipotle peppers add heat to food from Mexico, Central America, and the American Southwest. Canned chipotles in adobo are packed in a sauce with tomatoes, vinegar, and other spices. Canned chipotles pack quite a bit of heat, so use them sparingly. Once the can is open, store any chiles and sauce not being used in a lidded jar or container and refrigerate for up to two weeks. Ground chipotle

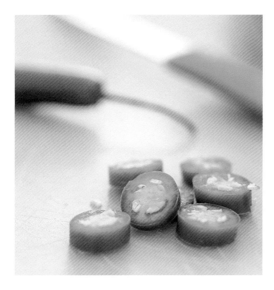

pepper is a dark rust red powder that is easily sprinkled on food.

Jalapeño peppers are sold fresh, canned, and pickled. Fresh ones can be green or red and range from mild to super-hot; it all depends how long they stayed on the vine and where they were grown. Canned jalapeños are generally mild while pickled ones are up there on the heat chart. If you can't find any other chiles, use jalapeños.

OILS

I try to cook with as little oil as possible. To limit the use of oil, a good set of nonstick cooking pans is a must. This way, you use your oil for flavor and not necessarily to assure your food does not stick. Not all oils are the same, so here are my go-to oils depending on the recipe.

Canola oil is my preferred vegetable oil when I want something neutral for sautéing aromatic vegetables like onions, carrots, and celery and for searing or browning chicken and meat. Canola oil is healthier than regular vegetable oil because it is lower in (bad) saturated fat and higher in (good) polyunsaturated and monounsaturated fats. Canola contains omega-3 fatty acids, essential for your well-being.

Cooking sprays, available in aerosol cans, really cut down on the amount of oil I cook with. Instead of brushing or oiling pans or baking dishes with oil, I spray them with a light film. Again, canola oil is used for most of my cooking, but occasionally I spray olive oil or butter-flavored oil. Choose the one(s) that suit you best.

Olive oil is my go-to oil for sautéing, dressing, and finishing food. I use regular olive oil for cooking, but feel free to use an inexpensive brand of extra-virgin olive oil. I save the best quality extra-virgin olive oils that I carry back from Spain or South America to drizzle on soups, salads or steamed vegetables. Since olive oils range in taste from grassy to peppery, find one that suits your palate.

VINEGARS

I now use more vinegar than ever as a condiment in my cooking, so I keep several different kinds in my pantry. Adding a splash of red wine or balsamic vinegar will perk up any pan sauce without adding any fat or many calories. When making salad dressings, use white or regular balsamic, champagne, or sherry vinegars.

Apple cider vinegar: Inexpensive and readily available, use in marinades and salad dressings.

Balsamic vinegar: Made from unfermented grape juice, Italian balsamic ranges widely in price depending on how long it's been aged. Use the mildly acidic, dark balsamic vinegar available in supermarkets for marinades and pan sauces, and even on top of fruit.

Champagne vinegar: Light and mild, use it to flavor beans or dress delicate lettuces.

Fruit-infused vinegars: Delicious on steamed vegetables and in fruit sauces, they're less harsh than others so you can use more vinegar and less oil in salad dressings.

Sherry wine vinegar: Use Spanish sherry wine vinegar in dressings, marinades, and sauces when you want a more assertive flavor.

White balsamic vinegar: I use this clear vinegar when I want a bit of balsamic flavor, but not the dark color, on fruits and in salad dressings.

sunny fried eggs and avocado quesadillas

pillow talk
and power up

(2)

Mom was always right: Breakfast *is* the most important meal of the day. It fires you up in the morning and kick-starts your metabolism to take on the day. I am a breakfast person; I always wake up hungry and have never been able to skip the first meal.

As much as I'd love to eat a lavish breakfast every morning, I don't have much time. Most days, I'm out of the house by five a.m. for TV tapings and live segments or running to catch a plane. Call me a little *loca*, but I confess I love having last night's leftovers—like steak—first thing in the morning. But on those busy mornings when I'm still half asleep but need to whip up some sustenance, I rely on quickies, such as a parfait layered with fruit and yogurt, eggs and vegetables "scrambled" in the microwave, egg white pancakes, or a sunny-side-up fried egg and avocado quesadilla. These simple recipes mean you'll never have an excuse for passing up a homemade breakfast.

Weekends allow me to prepare breakfast favorites that take a little more time. And they're worth it. I might bake some Cinnamon-*Pepita* Muffins or "drown" (poach) some eggs in a chipotle-tomato sauce.

Whether you wake up craving something quick and light or leisurely and substantial, you'll find plenty of morning ideas to get you going.

fluffy egg white pancakes with papaya-banana compote

When I'm craving pancakes, I make what I call my miracle pancakes. They contain no flour, so they're gluten- and starch-free. They're packed with protein—not fat—since only egg whites are used. The naturally sweet fruit compote takes the place of cloying maple syrup. They're easy to make and truly a miracle.

MAKES 2 SERVINGS

1 ripe banana, mashed

1 cup ripe papaya, mashed

1 tablespoon lime juice

6 large egg whites

1 teaspoon vanilla extract

freshly grated zest of 1 lime

olive oil cooking spray

toasted sweetened coconut flakes (optional)

1. Mash the banana and papaya with the lime juice and set aside.

2. Beat the egg whites with an electric hand mixer on high speed just until they hold soft peaks. Do not overmix. Fold in the vanilla and half of the lime zest.

3. Heat a small nonstick skillet over medium heat and spray with the olive oil. Ladle ½ cup of the egg whites mixture onto the heated skillet and swirl around as you would when making a crepe. Cook until there are small holes on top and the pancake is firm enough to flip over (about 1 minute). Cook the second side for under a minute or until set.

4. Serve the pancakes with some of the papaya-and-banana mixture on the side. Sprinkle with the remaining lime zest and toasted coconut flakes. Serve immediately.

CHICA TIP

To toast coconut flakes, spread the coconut on a baking sheet and bake in a preheated 300°F oven, stirring occasionally, until very lightly browned, about 8 minutes.

17

pillow talk and power up

cinnamon-*pepita* muffins

That enticing muffin at your local coffee bar probably contains 500—or more—calories! Why not make these healthful low-fat muffins instead? Applesauce and egg whites replace the fat in oil and whole eggs. Buttermilk—also low in fat—gives baked goods a soft texture and a tangy flavor. And toasted pumpkin seeds add some crunch. Bake a batch and keep them in the freezer. Pop one in the toaster oven in the morning while the coffee is brewing.

MAKES 12 MUFFINS

cooking spray

1 cup all-purpose flour

1 cup whole-wheat flour

2 teaspoons ground cinnamon

1 teaspoon baking powder

1 teaspoon baking soda

½ teaspoon salt

½ cup unsweetened applesauce

4 large egg whites

1½ cups buttermilk

1 teaspoon vanilla extract

½ cup old-fashioned (rolled) oats

½ cup packed light brown sugar

½ cup unsalted pumpkin seeds (*pepitas*), toasted

1. Preheat the oven to 400°F. Spray a 12-cup muffin pan with cooking spray.

2. Sift the all-purpose flour, whole-wheat flour, cinnamon, baking powder, baking soda, and salt together. Set aside.

3. With an electric mixer, mix the applesauce, egg whites, buttermilk, and vanilla on low speed until combined. Add half of the flour mixture and mix until smooth. Add the oats, brown sugar, and pumpkin seeds with the remaining flour mixture and mix until smooth.

4. Divide the batter evenly among the cups. Bake until a tester inserted into the center of a muffin comes out clean, about 15 minutes. Let cool at room temperature for 5 minutes. Remove from the cups and let cool on a wire cooling rack.

mixed berries and lime crema parfaits

Layer some berries and yogurt flavored with honey and lime in tall parfait glasses, and they become more than just berries and yogurt. While they're great for a quick breakfast, I also make these parfaits when I want dessert. Sometime I substitute a drop or two of stevia in place of the honey.

MAKES 4 SERVINGS

3 cups nonfat plain Greek yogurt

1 tablespoon honey

¾ teaspoon finely grated lime zest

1 tablespoon fresh lime juice

1½ teaspoons vanilla extract

1 cup fresh raspberries

1 cup fresh blueberries

1 cup fresh quartered strawberries

mint leaves for garnish

1. In a medium bowl, whisk together the yogurt, honey, lime zest, lime juice, and vanilla. Refrigerate until ready to make the parfaits.

2. Starting with the berries, alternately layer the fruit and yogurt in tall glasses. Garnish with mint leaves before serving.

Note: For an attractive presentation, layer the parfait ingredients in small mason jars.

CHICA TIP

Unsweetened cocoa powder is known to have properties that fight hunger pangs and reduce food cravings. When those cravings kick in between meals, stir a tablespoon of unsweetened cocoa powder into a cup of nonfat yogurt. If you need a bit more sweetness, add a drop or two of stevia.

drowned spicy mexican eggs
(huevos ahogados)

Huevos Ahogados, which means "drowned eggs," is a Mexican classic. They're poached—drowned—in a smoky tomato and chipotle chile sauce, then garnished with crumbled *queso fresco* and served with warm corn tortillas to sop up every bit. *Huevos Ahogados* are great for breakfast, but you can also enjoy them on a bed of cooked rice, steamed asparagus, or other vegetables for lunch or dinner.

MAKES 2 SERVINGS

2 pounds tomatoes, coarsely chopped

¼ cup fresh cilantro, plus more for garnish, coarsely chopped

¼ medium yellow onion, coarsely chopped

2 garlic cloves, coarsely chopped

1 teaspoon chipotle powder

1 tablespoon canola or vegetable oil

kosher salt

4 large eggs

4 corn tortillas, toasted

1 ripe Hass avocado, peeled, pitted, and sliced

½ cup crumbled *queso fresco*

CHICA TIP

To toast tortillas, place on a baking sheet and spray with canola oil. Bake in a preheated 400°F oven for 5 minutes. Turn the tortillas, spray the other sides, and continue baking until crisp, about 10 minutes.

1. In a blender or food processor, puree the tomatoes, cilantro, onion, garlic, and chipotle powder, adding a little bit of water as needed. Puree until you have a thin sauce.

2. Heat a medium skillet over medium-high heat. Add the cooking oil to the pan and heat until shimmering. Add the tomato sauce—be careful because it will spatter—and boil, stirring occasionally, until slightly thickened, about 3 minutes. Season with salt.

3. One at a time, crack each egg into a ramekin and slowly add the egg to the sauce. Continue with the other eggs. Turn the heat down to low, cover, and cook for about 6 to 7 minutes for eggs with soft yolks or 10 minutes for fully cooked eggs.

4. For each serving, place a tortilla on a plate; top with an egg and a quarter of the sauce. Top each with avocado slices and a sprinkle of the cilantro and *queso fresco*.

Variations:
- Poach the eggs in jarred salsa verde and top them with some sliced avocado.
- When fresh, ripe tomatoes are out of season, substitute one 28-ounce can of crushed tomatoes.

sunny fried eggs and avocado quesadillas

Think quesadillas for breakfast, not just for lunch or as appetizers. Change up the fillings depending on what's in your refrigerator. Leftover chicken? Turkey? Cooked vegetables? For a vegan version, omit the egg and add lettuce leaves. To finish, I drizzle some extra-virgin olive oil on top. Ezekiel or another whole-grain bread can be used in place of tortillas.

MAKES 2 SERVINGS

1 teaspoon olive oil

2 large eggs

2 large whole-grain tortillas

1 ripe Hass avocado, peeled, seeded, and mashed

1 medium tomato, sliced

1 tablespoon pine nuts or pumpkin seeds (*pepitas*)

2 tablespoons fresh cilantro, chopped

½ jalapeño, seeded and thinly sliced (optional)

extra-virgin olive oil for drizzling

kosher salt

freshly ground black pepper

1. Brush a small nonstick skillet with the oil and heat over medium heat. Add the eggs one at a time and cook sunny side up about 2 minutes. Using a spatula, transfer to a plate.

2. While the eggs are cooking, warm the tortillas in a separate skillet (no need to add any oil).

3. For each serving, spread a tortilla with half of the mashed avocado, tomatoes, pine nuts, cilantro, and jalapeños, if using. Top with an egg, drizzle with extra-virgin olive oil, and season with salt and pepper. Fold over and serve.

latin d'lite

zippy quick three-minute egg scramble in a cup

My all-time favorite and almost daily go-to breakfast! I whisk an egg and egg whites together with whatever vegetables I have on hand in a coffee cup, then pop it into the microwave for 2½ minutes. I make this so often that I'm sure I could put it together in my sleep.

MAKES 1 SERVING

1 large egg plus 2 egg whites

¼ cup frozen chopped spinach

¼ cup roasted red peppers, chopped

pinch of dry oregano or a sprinkle of chopped fresh flat-leaf parsley

kosher salt

freshly ground black pepper, to taste

1 tablespoon shredded mozzarella

1 teaspoon freshly grated Parmesan

1. In a microwave-safe cup, beat the egg and egg whites with the spinach, red peppers, and oregano. Season with salt and pepper. Sprinkle the mozzarella on top.

2. Place the cup in the microwave and cook on high, uncovered, for 2½ minutes. As it cooks, the egg mixture will rise above the rim of the cup like a soufflé. (Since microwave ovens are different from one another, check after the above cooking time to see that the eggs rose properly. If not, return to the microwave for another 20 seconds.) Remove from the microwave and sprinkle with the Parmesan.

CHICA TIP

! Instead of spinach, stir in some frozen corn kernels with ½ teaspoon tapenade, black beans, and diced tomato, or a teaspoon of pesto.

plantains-and-peppers frittata

Instead of potatoes as an accompaniment to egg–and-vegetable omelets and frittatas, add some ripe plantains to the mix. Plantains are packed with antioxidants and are cooked here in far less fat than fried potatoes.

MAKES 4 SERVINGS

3 teaspoons olive oil, divided

1 ripe plantain, peeled and sliced in ¼-inch-thick rounds

1 medium yellow onion, chopped

1 red bell pepper, seeded and chopped

2 garlic cloves, minced

4 large eggs plus 2 large egg whites

1 tablespoon fresh cilantro, chopped

¼ teaspoon salt

¼ teaspoon hot sauce

¼ cup part-skim ricotta cheese

CHICA TIP

! Plantains look like big bananas, but they're firmer, starchier, and less sweet than "dessert" bananas. Plantains can be unripe and green or ripe and sweet. In either case, they should be cooked, rather than eaten raw like bananas.

1. Heat 1 teaspoon of oil in a medium ovenproof nonstick skillet over medium-high heat. Add the plantains and cook, turning occasionally, until browned, about 4 minutes. Transfer the plantains to a plate.

2. Heat the remaining 2 teaspoons oil in the skillet. Add the onion, bell pepper, and garlic and cook over medium heat, stirring occasionally, until the vegetables are very tender, 12 to 14 minutes.

3. Adjust the broiler rack 5 to 7 inches from the heat and preheat the broiler.

4. Whisk together the eggs, egg whites, cilantro, salt, and hot sauce in a large bowl. Pour the egg mixture evenly over the vegetable mixture. Tuck the plantains into the egg-vegetable mixture. Cook over medium heat, tilting the pan and lifting the edges with a rubber spatula to let the uncooked egg flow underneath, just until the eggs are barely set around the edges. Spoon the ricotta over the frittata. Broil until the frittata is puffed and golden around the edges, about 5 minutes. Cut into wedges and serve.

breakfast burritos with cilantro-*pepita* salsa

When my friends come for a weekend brunch, I serve these burritos filled with eggs, black beans, and tomatoes and top them with some cilantro–pumpkin seed salsa. I always make a double batch of the salsa to accompany grilled chicken, beef, or pork during the rest of the week.

MAKES 4 SERVINGS

salsa:

2 cups roughly chopped fresh cilantro

½ cup hulled pumpkin seeds (*pepitas*), toasted

½ cup water

1 small shallot, finely minced

1 tablespoon honey

1 garlic clove, finely minced

kosher salt

freshly ground black pepper

burritos:

4 large eggs

1 cup tomatoes, chopped

1 tablespoon jalapeño, seeded and finely chopped

kosher salt and freshly ground black pepper

4 12-inch whole-wheat tortillas

1 15-ounce can black beans, rinsed and drained

1 cup shredded mozzarella

toasted pumpkin seeds (*pepitas*) for garnish

1. To make the salsa, combine all of the salsa ingredients except the salt and pepper in a food processor. Pulse until chunky. Pour into a bowl and season with salt and pepper. Set aside.

2. To make the burritos, heat a nonstick skillet over medium heat. Whisk the eggs in a bowl. Add the chopped tomatoes and jalapeño. Pour into the skillet and cook, stirring occasionally, until the eggs are cooked to desired doneness. Season with salt and pepper.

3. Wrap the tortillas in damp paper towels. Microwave on high for 20 seconds to warm them and make them pliable for rolling.

4. Heat a large griddle or frying pan over medium heat. Divide the scrambled eggs among the tortillas. Top with 2 tablespoons of black beans, 2 tablespoons cheese, and 1 tablespoon salsa. Fold in 2 sides, then roll up from the bottom. Cook on the griddle, turning once, until both sides are lightly browned and crispy, about 1 to 2 minutes per side.

5. To serve, cut each burrito in half on the diagonal. Drizzle with some of the remaining salsa, sprinkle with pumpkin seeds, and serve immediately.

torrijas

Torrijas, or Spanish-style French toast, are eaten throughout Spain at Easter. The classic version calls for bread to be fried in olive oil and then dipped in wine, honey, and cinnamon. I dip the bread in the traditional honey and cinnamon mixed with a bit of espresso for a mocha flavor.

MAKES 4 SERVINGS

4 large egg whites

2 tablespoons brewed espresso or 1 teaspoon instant espresso dissolved in 2 tablespoons boiling water (optional)

1 tablespoon honey

1 teaspoon vanilla extract

⅛ teaspoon ground cinnamon

cooking spray

8 slices honey-wheat bread

2 ripe bananas, sliced

½ cup nonfat plain Greek yogurt or kefir

1. Preheat the oven to 200°F. Whisk the egg whites, espresso (if using), honey, vanilla, and cinnamon together in a large bowl until well combined.

2. Spray a large nonstick skillet with cooking spray and heat over medium heat. In batches, dip the bread in the egg mixture, making sure to cover all sides. Place the bread in the skillet and cook until the underside is golden brown, about 3 minutes. Flip the bread over and cook until the other side is golden brown, about 3 minutes more. Transfer the *torrijas* to a platter and keep warm in the oven.

3. Mash the banana in a bowl with a fork. Mix in the yogurt.

4. Serve the *torrijas* warm topped by the banana-yogurt mixture.

pillow talk and power up

energizing *batidos*

Batidos, the Latin American version of smoothies, are usually made with milk and fruit. I prefer nutrient-rich kefir, a fermented milk drink much like a thin yogurt. This energy-boosting meal in a glass is perfect for breakfast, after a workout, or when that midafternoon slump hits. *Batidos* are incredibly versatile; make them with any kind of fruit you have on hand. For extra protein, add a tablespoon of peanut or almond butter. You can also use almond or coconut milk in place of the kefir.

MAKES 2 SERVINGS

1 banana, quartered and frozen

½ cup frozen mango cubes

½ cup blueberries, plus more for garnish

1 cup nonfat plain kefir

⅛ teaspoon vanilla extract

1 1-inch piece of fresh ginger, peeled and grated

2 tablespoons flaxseed meal

2 fresh mint sprigs for garnish

Put all of the ingredients, except the mint, in a blender and puree until smooth. Pour immediately into chilled tall glasses. Garnish with a few berries and mint sprigs before serving.

CHICA TIP

As soon as my bananas, strawberries, mangoes, and other fruit start to become overripe, I cut them up and freeze them in zip-top plastic bags. In the morning, when I'm in a hurry, I don't have to spend time cutting up fruit to make a *batido*. And frozen fruit means you don't have to add any ice.

mom's creamy fruit salad

Pineapple, apple, and melons are tossed with toasted coconut, plain yogurt, and a good dose of rum in this fruit salad. My mom often put a bowl of this grown-ups-only salad on her holiday dinner table to accompany ham or turkey. While Mom made it with heavy cream, I prefer mine made with nonfat Greek yogurt. Serve it with a meal in place of a green salad, or for a quick dessert, or layer the fruit and other ingredients in martini glasses for a stunning brunch presentation.

MAKES 6 TO 8 SERVINGS

1 cup nonfat Greek yogurt

¼ cup dark or spiced rum

3 tablespoons honey

2 tablespoons finely chopped fresh mint leaves

½ small pineapple, peeled, cored, and chopped

2 apples (Gala, Granny Smith, or Fuji), cored and chopped

¼ small watermelon, peeled, seeded, and chopped

½ cantaloupe or honeydew melon, peeled, seeded, and chopped

1 cup sweetened coconut flakes, toasted (see *Chica Tip* page 17)

1. Whisk together yogurt, rum, honey, and mint in a small bowl.

2. Mix together the pineapple, apples, watermelon, and cantaloupe in a large bowl. Add the dressing, toss, and let stand for 10 minutes. Sprinkle on the coconut before serving.

Indulge!
eggs in baskets

For a stunning brunch presentation, fill flaky mini cups of filo dough with some Mexican chorizo and onion hash and crown with a sunny-side-up egg.

MAKES 4 SERVINGS

cooking spray

1 tablespoon olive oil

½ pound fresh chorizo, casings removed and chopped

1 medium yellow onion, chopped

8 9 x 14–inch sheets frozen filo dough, thawed

8 large eggs

1. Preheat the oven to 350°F. Spray four 7-inch round individual baking dishes with cooking spray.

2. Heat the oil in a large nonstick skillet over medium-high heat. Add the sausage and onion and cook, stirring occasionally, until the onion is tender and the sausage is browned, 6 to 8 minutes. Remove from the heat; set aside.

3. Place 2 filo sheets on a clean, dry surface. (Cover the remaining filo with a clean towel to keep it from drying out.) Lightly spray each sheet with nonstick spray; then stack one sheet on top of the other. Repeat with the remaining filo, making a total of 4 stacks.

4. For each serving, gently ease a stack into the prepared baking dishes, pressing the filo against the bottom of the dish. Spoon ¼ cup of the sausage mixture into each dish; then break two eggs on top. Crimp the edges of the filo so they slightly cover the eggs.

5. Place the dishes on a large baking sheet. Bake until the filo is crisp and the eggs are just set, 10 to 15 minutes. Serve at once.

tropical caprese salad
with cilantro aïoli

appeteasers, snacks, and dippidy-do dips

3

Appetizers may be my favorite part of a meal. When I don't feel like cooking a complete lunch or dinner or can't decide what I want to eat, I often make two or three appetizers, or as I like to call them "appeteasers." These small treats allow me to enjoy a variety of flavors and textures.

The most up-to-date nutritional and dietary research shows that eating smaller, more frequent meals—breakfast, lunch, and dinner with two healthy snacks—before real hunger pangs set in is one of the most important keys to successful weight management. If you wait until you're ravenous to eat, you'll overeat. If you wait too long between meals and snacks, then you'll find yourself reaching for the first thing available—cookies, potato chips, or brownies. Plan ahead and take your own snacks to work or school. When traveling, taking along some Salt-and-Vinegar Kale Chips, Chili-Spiced Popcorn, or a 3½-ounce container of Smoky Roasted Poblano and Garbanzo Dip with some cut-up vegetables is just as essential as packing my makeup. With my own treats stashed in my carry-on bag, I just keep walking past all the airport junk food and know that I have some healthy snacks to get me through the trip.

My Dippidy-Do Dips are time-savers and calorie savers! They can be made ahead and stored in the refrigerator, which is great when entertaining. They're low in calories and fat, but sky-high on flavor.

spanish tomato toast
(*pan tumaca*)

Sometimes the simplest foods are the best, like this popular tomato bread from Catalonia in Spain. Oven-crisped bread slices are rubbed with a garlic clove and then half a tomato. The bread absorbs the garlic's essence and the sunny flavors of ripe tomatoes. That's it. Using a good loaf of bread, your fruitiest olive oil, and the best kosher salt makes all the difference.

MAKES 4 SERVINGS

1 8-ounce whole-wheat baguette, cut into 8 ½-inch-thick slices

4 garlic cloves, halved

4 plum tomatoes, halved

¼ cup extra-virgin olive oil

¾ teaspoon kosher salt

¾ teaspoon freshly ground black pepper

1. Preheat the oven to 425°F. Put the bread slices on a baking sheet. Bake until golden, 8 to 10 minutes. Transfer the bread slices to a cutting board to cool slightly.

2. When the bread is cool enough to handle, rub both sides of each slice with a half clove of garlic. Rub each bread slice with a tomato half, pressing firmly to push the pulp into the bread. Discard the skins and remaining pulp. Drizzle the oil over the bread. Sprinkle with the salt and pepper and serve.

CHICA TIP

Tomato bread makes a great base for other toppings—roasted red peppers, a slice of Manchego cheese or serrano ham, Spanish *boquerones* (white anchovies) or sardines, or Avocadolicious Dip (page 63). Set out bowls of olives and Marcona almonds and vases filled with bread sticks. All you need are pitchers of red and white sangria and you have an instant tapas party.

appeteasers, snacks, and dippidy-do dips

zucchini *tiradito* carpaccio

I first tasted this zucchini carpaccio, which in Spanish is called *tiradito*, on a summer visit to Tuscany. I recall thinking, "How strange, raw zucchini?" I loved the delicate buttery flavor instantly. In Italy, paper-thin zucchini is gently tossed with olive oil, lemon juice, and herbs, but I add a Latina twist and sprinkle in some crumbled *queso blanco* and cilantro.

MAKES 6 TO 8 SERVINGS

zest of 1 Meyer (or regular if not available) lemon, freshly grated

¼ cup fresh Meyer (or regular) lemon juice

¼ cup olive oil

kosher salt

fresh ground black pepper

3 green or yellow zucchini, trimmed

1 tablespoon fresh cilantro, finely chopped

1 tablespoon fresh chives, finely chopped

1 tablespoon fresh dill, finely chopped

½ cup *queso blanco* or reduced-fat feta, crumbled

1. Whisk the lemon zest and juice in a small bowl. Gradually whisk in the oil. Season with salt and pepper and whisk again. Cover and refrigerate to blend the flavors, about 15 minutes.

2. Using a mandoline, slice the zucchini into very thin, ¹⁄₁₆-inch rounds.

3. Mix the cilantro, chives, and dill together in a small bowl. Layer the zucchini rounds on a platter, seasoning each layer with salt and pepper. Pour the olive oil mixture on top and move plate around to make sure liquid distributes evenly. Sprinkle with the crumbled cheese and mixed herbs. Serve immediately.

CHICA TIP

! **No matter how good your knife skills, owning a mandoline that slices and juliennes fruit, vegetables, and other ingredients is a must. Professional mandolines are expensive, about $150, but I prefer the reasonably priced Joyce Chen Asian Mandoline Plus.**

chorizo-stuffed mushrooms

Chorizo, uncooked pork sausage with spices, is a traditional Mexican ingredient, but a lot of its flavor comes from pork fat. Fortunately, a little bit of chorizo goes a long way when it comes to adding big flavors to these stuffed mushrooms. Since portobellos are large, serve one to each guest for an impressive first course.

MAKES 6 SERVINGS

cooking spray

6 4-inch portobello mushrooms, stems removed

1 tablespoon olive oil

2 medium yellow onions, chopped

3 ounces raw Mexican chorizo, with casings removed and crumbled

2 slices soft whole-wheat bread, crusts trimmed and discarded, and torn

1 2-ounce piece reduced-fat pepper Jack cheese

¼ teaspoon kosher salt

¼ teaspoon freshly ground black pepper

1. Preheat the oven to 375°F. Spray a medium baking sheet with nonstick spray.

2. Chop 2 of the mushrooms. Place the remaining 4 mushrooms on the baking sheet.

3. Heat the oil in a large nonstick skillet over medium heat. Add the chopped mushroom caps, onions, and chorizo. Cook, stirring occasionally, breaking up the chorizo with the side of a spoon, until the mushroom caps are very tender, 10 to 12 minutes.

4. Pulse the bread slices in a food processor until fine crumbs form. Transfer to a small bowl. Add the cheese to the food processor and pulse until finely chopped. Add to the bread crumbs, mix well, and season with salt and pepper.

5. Spoon equal amounts of the chorizo mixture into the mushroom caps and sprinkle evenly with the bread crumb mixture. Lightly spray the tops with cooking spray. Bake until the filling is hot and the topping is lightly browned, about 30 minutes.

6. Serve hot.

turkey nachos

Yes, you can make—and enjoy—healthy nachos! I cut up and bake whole-wheat tortillas and cover them with cooked ground turkey, black beans, and a light sprinkle of reduced-fat Mexican cheese blend. Avocado, scallions, and nonfat Greek yogurt add the final touches.

pico de gallo:

4 small ripe tomatoes, diced

1 small white onion, diced

2 jalapeño peppers, seeded and finely chopped

½ cup packed cilantro leaves, chopped

¼ cup fresh lime juice

1 teaspoon extra-virgin olive oil

kosher salt

freshly ground black pepper

filling:

2 tablespoons olive oil

1 pound ground lean turkey breast

1½ teaspoons chili powder

1 teaspoon ground cumin

½ teaspoon garlic powder

½ teaspoon onion powder

½ teaspoon sweet paprika

¼ teaspoon dried oregano

⅛ teaspoon salt

¼ cup water

nachos:

4 8- to 10-inch whole-wheat or whole-grain tortillas, each cut into 6 wedges

cooking spray

1 8-ounce bag shredded reduced-fat Mexican cheese blend

1 15-ounce can black beans, rinsed and drained

½ cup ripe black olives, sliced

1 Hass avocado, peeled, halved, pitted, and diced

low-fat sour cream or nonfat plain Greek yogurt (optional)

2 scallions, white and green parts, chopped (½ cup)

1. To make the pico de gallo, combine the tomatoes, onion, jalapeños, cilantro, lime juice, and oil together in a medium bowl. Season with salt and pepper.

2. For the filling, heat the oil in a large skillet over medium-high heat. Add the turkey and the chili power, cumin, garlic powder, onion powder, paprika, oregano, and salt. Cook, stirring often, breaking up the turkey with the side of a spoon, until the turkey begins to brown, about 5 minutes. Stir in the water and reduce the heat to medium-low. Cover and simmer until the turkey is cooked through, about 5 minutes.

3. Preheat the oven to 400°F. Line 2 large baking sheets with aluminum foil.

4. Spread the tortilla wedges on the baking sheets and spray with the nonstick spray. Bake until golden brown and crispy, about 5 minutes. Remove from the oven.

5. Spray a large, shallow baking dish with nonstick spray. Spread half of the tortilla wedges in the baking dish, and top with half of the cheese, half of the turkey mixture, half of the beans, and half of the olives. Top with remaining tortilla wedges, and repeat with the remaining cheese, turkey mixture, beans, and olives. Bake until the cheese melts, about 10 minutes.

6. Remove from oven and sprinkle with half of the pico de gallo and the avocado. Spoon a large dollop of the sour cream on top of the nachos. Sprinkle with the scallions. Serve immediately, with the remaining pico de gallo on the side.

sardine antipasto tostadas

As long as I have some canned sardines and capers in my pantry, I know I can put this simple Spanish-inspired appetizer together for guests or for a quick meal for myself. I top toasted and garlic-rubbed bread with sardines, a tomato-caper-onion salad, and a few arugula leaves. Arrange the tostadas on a platter and serve with cava, Spanish sparkling wine. My favorite sardines are Ortiz brand from Spain, which are available in many markets or online at Latienda.com.

MAKES 4 TO 6 SERVINGS

2 large tomatoes, seeded and cut into ½ inch dice

2 tablespoons drained nonpareil capers

grated zest of 1 lemon

1 tablespoon fresh lemon juice

1 tablespoon red onion, finely chopped

1 tablespoon fresh flat-leaf parsley, plus more for garnish, finely chopped

1 tablespoon olive oil

⅛ teaspoon ground cumin

salt

freshly ground black pepper

1 whole-wheat French baguette, cut on the diagonal into 12 to 14 ½-inch slices

1 garlic clove, halved

1 6.7-ounce can of sardines in oil, drained and shredded with a fork

2 cups baby arugula

extra-virgin olive oil

1. Combine the tomatoes, capers, ¼ of the lemon zest, lemon juice, onion, parsley, oil, and cumin. Season with salt and pepper.

2. Preheat the oven to 500°F. Arrange the bread slices on a large baking sheet. Bake for 2 minutes. Flip the bread slices over and bake until the bread is lightly toasted, about 2 minutes more. While the toast is still warm, rub each slice with the garlic clove halves.

3. Top each toast with an equal amount of shredded sardines, the tomato mixture, and a few arugula leaves. Arrange on a serving platter. Drizzle with the extra-virgin olive oil. Sprinkle with the remaining lemon zest and parsley and season with salt and pepper. Serve immediately.

CHICA TIP

! Tostada means any bread—tortillas or sliced loaves—that has been toasted. Any leftover bread or tostadas can be used in *Torrijas* (page 29) or ground into bread crumbs.

tropical caprese salad with cilantro aïoli

Juicy pineapple and mango replace mozzarella in my tropical version of insalata Caprese. Not only do the natural bromelain enzymes in the fruit aid in digestion, but the sweet-and-tart pineapple balances the flavors in this salad.

aïoli:

¼ cup packed coarsely chopped fresh cilantro

2 large egg yolks

2 garlic cloves, peeled

⅛ teaspoon salt

¼ cup olive oil

salad:

4 large tomatoes, cut into ½ inch-thick rounds

1¼ cups diced fresh pineapple

1½ cups diced fresh mango

3 fresh basil leaves, thinly sliced

1. To make the cilantro aïoli, puree the cilantro, egg yolks, garlic, and salt in a food processor or blender. With the machine running, drizzle in the oil through the feed tube (or the hole in the lid of a blender) until thickened and creamy.

2. Divide the tomato rounds evenly among 6 plates. Top evenly with the pineapple and diced mango and sprinkle with the basil. Drizzle each with the cilantro aïoli. Serve immediately.

CHICA TIP

!

- **If you're concerned about consuming raw eggs, in-the-shell pasteurized eggs are now available in many supermarkets.**
- **Don't throw away those pineapple skins! Pineapple has long been known for its diuretic and anti-inflammatory effects. Put the cut-up skin of a pineapple and 1 quart of water in a pot. Bring to a boil and then turn off the heat. Let steep for 4 to 6 hours. Strain in a container and refrigerate up to 2 days. I drink a glass to get rid of bloat or when I'm feeling a little achy.**

black beans and *queso fresco* five-grain tostadas

I toast slices of whole-grain bread for healthier tostadas. (Whole-grain breads contain twice as much dietary fiber and protein as white breads.) I top them with creamy black beans, cherry tomatoes, and a bit of *queso fresco* for an easy appetizer. Stir in some canned tuna for main course open-faced tostadas.

MAKES 6 SERVINGS

1 whole-wheat French baguette, cut on the diagonal into 14 ½-inch slices

1 garlic clove, peeled and cut in half

1 teaspoon olive oil, plus more for drizzling

1 15-ounce can black beans, drained and rinsed

2 teaspoons red wine vinegar

⅛ teaspoon sweet paprika

⅛ teaspoon salt

1 cup grape or cherry tomatoes, finely chopped

2 tablespoons fresh cilantro, plus more for garnish, finely chopped

½ cup *queso fresco* or reduced-fat feta, finely diced

freshly ground black pepper

1. Preheat the oven to 500°F.

2. Arrange the bread slices on a large baking sheet. Bake for 2 minutes. Flip the bread slices over and bake until the bread is lightly toasted, about 2 minutes more. While the toast is still warm, rub each slice with the garlic clove halves.

3. Heat the oil in a large skillet over medium-high heat. Add the black beans, vinegar, paprika, and salt and cook, stirring often, until hot, about 5 minutes. Stir in the tomatoes, cilantro, and half of the *queso fresco* and heat through, about 3 minutes more. Remove from the heat and season with the pepper.

4. To serve, top each toast with about 1 tablespoon of the black bean mixture and sprinkle with the remaining *queso fresco* and cilantro. Drizzle with olive oil and serve immediately.

CHICA TIP

! Queso fresco, or fresh cheese, with its slightly salty-tangy flavor and crumbly texture, is the go-to cheese in many Mexican dishes. *Queso fresco* softens but doesn't melt when heated, so it's ideal for using in quesadillas or enchiladas and for sprinkling on soups, salads, and tostadas. If you can't find *queso fresco*, use a reduced-fat feta.

baked codfish balls *(bolas de bacalao)*

My light and airy baked codfish balls are an entirely different kettle of fish from the fried ones my mother made with salt cod. I use fresh cod, which doesn't require the time-consuming method of soaking and changing water like salted and dried cod. I find that green Tabasco has a milder flavor than the red.

MAKES 12 SERVINGS

- 3 medium baking potatoes, such as russets (1½ pounds), peeled and cut into chunks
- 3 cups bottled clam juice or fish stock
- 1 medium yellow onion, quartered
- 1 bay leaf
- 1 pound cod or haddock fillets, cut into 2-inch pieces
- 2 large eggs, lightly beaten
- 3 tablespoons fresh cilantro, plus more for garnish, finely chopped
- 1½ teaspoons green hot sauce, such as Tabasco
- 1 teaspoon kosher salt
- cooking spray
- 1 cup seasoned dry bread crumbs

1. Put the potatoes and clam juice in a medium saucepan and bring to a boil over medium heat. Reduce the heat to medium-low, cover, and cook until the potatoes are fork tender, about 20 minutes. Using a slotted spoon, transfer the potatoes to a bowl. Do not discard the cooking liquid. While the potatoes are still hot, mash them with a hand masher and set aside.

2. Add the onion and bay leaf to the cooking liquid. Bring to a simmer over low heat and cook for 3 minutes. Add the cod to the simmering broth and cook until the fish is opaque, about 3 minutes. Remove the fish with a slotted spoon and add to the mashed potatoes. Mix well.

3. Add the eggs, cilantro, hot sauce, and salt to the fish-and-potato mixture. Mix until well combined. Cover with plastic wrap and refrigerate until completely cooled and firm, at least 4 hours or preferably overnight.

4. Preheat the oven to 400°F. Coat a baking sheet with nonstick cooking spray. Spread the bread crumbs on a plate.

5. Using a small ice-cream scoop, roll the chilled fish-and-potato mixture into 2-inch balls. Then roll each ball in bread crumbs to coat completely. Put the codfish balls on the prepared pan and spray the tops lightly with nonstick cooking spray; this will make them really crispy. Bake until the codfish balls are nicely browned, 20 to 25 minutes. Transfer the codfish balls to a platter and sprinkle with cilantro.

CHICA TIP

! I often double this recipe and freeze a batch to keep on hand for unexpected guests and future parties. Shape and roll the cod balls in the bread crumbs, arrange them on a parchment paper–lined baking sheet, and put in the freezer. Once frozen, transfer them to a plastic bag. Defrost them overnight in the refrigerator or at room temperature before baking them.

appeteasers, snacks, and dippidy-do dips

bocaditos

I find that the easiest way to watch my weight is to look at a dish and ask, "What can I omit without sacrificing flavor?" I ditch the 200-calorie tortillas and wrap the fillings in romaine, Bibb, or other large lettuce leaves for satisfying *bocaditos*, or little bites. These little bites keep me from eating high-fat snacks with little nutritional value. Here are some of the other quick and filling *bocaditos* I enjoy:

TURKEY-WRAPPED AVOCADO: Wrap ¼ of an avocado with a thin slice of low-sodium turkey breast from the deli counter. Drizzle with ¼ teaspoon honey and sprinkle with crushed pistachios.

TURKEY LETTUCE ROLLITO WITH SOY CILANTRO YOGURT CREMA: Whisk together 2 tablespoons nonfat Greek yogurt, 1 teaspoon finely chopped fresh cilantro, ¼ teaspoon soy sauce (preferably Nama Shoyu), ½ teaspoon water, and a pinch of dried oregano in a small bowl. Spread the yogurt sauce on the lettuce leaves. Top with 2 thin slices of low-sodium turkey slices. Roll up and enjoy.

CHICA TIP

I purchase Applegate Farms Organic Naturals sliced turkey breast at the deli counter. It's real turkey roasted with a modest amount of salt and has no filler. I also recommend Nama Shoyu, a flavorful, unpasteurized soy sauce available at health food stores and many supermarkets.

chili-spiced popcorn

When I read that a large tub of movie theater salty popcorn can contain as much as 1,200 calories and 60 grams of saturated fat, I knew I had to create a healthier version. I cook popcorn in the smallest amount of good-for-you oil. Then, I give it a sassy zip with some Parmesan and a fine dusting of fiery chili powder and tart lime juice. Sit back and enjoy the movie!

MAKES 2 SERVINGS

1 tablespoon canola oil

¼ cup popcorn kernels

2 tablespoons freshly shredded Parmesan

1 teaspoon chili powder

salt

freshly ground black pepper

1 tablespoon finely chopped fresh cilantro

1. Heat the oil in a large, deep saucepan over high heat until very hot but not smoking. Add 1 popcorn kernel, cover tightly, and cook until it pops. Add the remaining popcorn, cover tightly, and cook, constantly moving the saucepan back and forth on the burner, until kernels stop popping, about 2 minutes.

2. Transfer the popcorn to a bowl. Add the Parmesan and chili powder and toss, seasoning with salt and pepper. Sprinkle with the cilantro and serve immediately.

appeteasers, snacks, and dippidy-do dips

salt-and-vinegar kale chips

Some people can't say no to anything with chocolate. My downfall is craving salt-and-vinegar potato chips in the afternoon. I needed to find something healthier but just as satisfying to hit the spot. For this healthy snack, I toss dark green kale leaves (be sure to use black, not curly, kale and dry the leaves well or they won't become crispy) with olive oil and vinegar and then bake them for a crispy treat. Kids and adults love these kale chips; you won't be able to make them fast enough.

1 bunch Tuscan kale (also called dinosaur, black kale, or *cavalo nero*), well washed and dried

1 tablespoon olive oil

1 tablespoon apple cider vinegar

kosher salt

1. Preheat the oven to 350°F. Line 2 large baking sheets with parchment paper.

2. Remove and discard the thick stems from the kale leaves. Cut the leaves into pieces about 3 inches long. Put the kale in a bowl and toss with the oil and vinegar. Spread on the baking sheets.

3. Bake until the leaves are crispy, about 15 minutes. Do not let the leaves color beyond dark green or they will taste bitter. Sprinkle with salt, carefully transfer to a bowl, and serve.

baked plantain chips

Fried plantain chips are the Hispanic equivalent of potato chips. Whether homemade or purchased, they're usually fried, making them an unhealthy choice. But baking plantain chips allows me to enjoy them more frequently. I serve them with dips and soups or as a satisfying snack by themselves.

MAKES 4 TO 6 SERVINGS

2 green plantains, peeled

3 tablespoons olive oil

kosher salt

1. Preheat the oven to 400°F. Line a large baking sheet with parchment paper or aluminum foil.

2. Using a mandoline or a knife, cut the plantains crosswise into 1/16-inch-thick rounds. Transfer to a medium bowl. Drizzle with the oil and toss to coat. Season with the salt. Spread in a single layer in the baking sheet.

3. Bake until the plantains are crispy and lightly browned, 18 to 20 minutes. Sprinkle with more salt, if desired.

mango-tomatillo guacamole

Think of guacamole as a blank canvas that takes well to the addition of other ingredients, like sweet mango and tart tomatillos. I serve this as a dip or as a sauce with grilled shrimp, fish, or chicken.

MAKES 2 CUPS

2 ripe Hass avocados, halved, seeded, and peeled

2 tomatillos, husked and finely chopped

1 ripe mango, peeled, seeded, and cubed

½ small red onion, finely chopped

1 serrano chile, finely chopped (remove seeds before chopping for less heat)

2 tablespoons fresh cilantro, chopped

1 tablespoon fresh mint leaves, chopped

1½ tablespoons fresh lemon juice

kosher salt

baked tortilla or pita chips, for serving

1. Mash the avocados in a medium bowl with a fork, leaving them still a bit chunky. Fold in the tomatillos, mango, onion, chile, cilantro, and mint. Add the lemon juice, and gently mix to evenly distribute the ingredients. Season with salt.

2. Lay a piece of plastic wrap directly on the surface of the guacamole to discourage discoloring, and refrigerate until chilled, at least 1 hour. Serve with the chips for dipping.

CHICA TIP

! Avocados are my go-to fruit, especially when it comes to maintaining my weight. I eat avocado at every meal, because it's healthy, filling, and, like all other fruits, has no saturated fat. I enjoy a few slices in the morning with scrambled egg whites, in main-course salads at lunch, and with fish or chicken at dinner. Spread some ripe avocado on whole-grain toast or use as a sandwich spread in place of mayonnaise. Between meals, snacking on half of a creamy avocado keeps me going. In particular, I enjoy Chilean Hass avocados for their intense flavors and rich textures. Look for them in your market.

smoky roasted poblano and garbanzo dip

This hummus-inspired chickpea dip replaces olive oil and high-fat tahini with thick Greek yogurt. What really makes it unique is the alluring smoky flavor of a roasted poblano pepper combined with caramelized garlic and musky cumin.

4 whole-wheat pitas, cut into 6 to 8 wedges

1 head garlic (see *Chica Tip* below)

1 poblano chile

extra-virgin olive oil

1 16-ounce can garbanzo beans (chickpeas), rinsed and drained

⅓ cup nonfat Greek yogurt

2 tablespoons fresh lime juice

2 tablespoons water, as needed

¼ teaspoon ground cumin

pinch of cayenne pepper

salt

freshly ground pepper

1. Preheat the oven to 375°F.

2. Spread the pita wedges on 2 baking sheets. Bake, flipping the wedges halfway through baking, until they are crisp, about 10 minutes. Transfer the wedges to a platter and let cool. Leave the oven on.

3. Line a baking sheet with aluminum foil. Following the Chica Tip below, place the foil-enclosed garlic on the baking sheet. Add the chile to the baking sheet and brush with oil. Bake, flipping the chile halfway through baking, until the chile skin is loosened and the garlic head feels soft when squeezed, about 30 minutes.

CHICA TIP

When roasted, garlic becomes slightly sweet and nutty and has a buttery texture. In fact, I now use roasted garlic in place of butter with grilled meats and baked vegetables.

Preheat the oven to 400°F. Rub off the outer layers of papery skin from a head—or two—of garlic. Slice ¼ inch off the top, exposing all of the garlic cloves. Place the whole head on a piece of aluminum foil large enough to enclose the garlic. Drizzle with olive oil and seal up the foil. Place the package on a small baking sheet and bake until soft when pierced with a knife, about 45 minutes to 1 hour. Remove and let cool. To use, squeeze the soft garlic out of each clove, discarding the skin. Cover and refrigerate any unused roasted garlic for up to 2 days.

latin d'lite

4. Transfer the chile to a small bowl and cover tightly with plastic wrap. Unwrap the garlic. Let stand at room temperature until cool enough to handle. Stem, seed, and skin the chile and put in a food processor. Squeeze the softened garlic flesh from the hulls into a small bowl. Add 2 roasted garlic cloves to the food processor, and cover and save the remaining garlic for another use.

5. Add the garbanzo beans, yogurt, lime juice, water, cumin, and cayenne pepper to the food processor and process until smooth. For a thinner dip, add more water, a tablespoon at a time. Season with salt and black pepper. Transfer the dip to a serving bowl. (The dip can be refrigerated for up to 2 days. Let stand at room temperature for 1 hour before serving.)

6. Drizzle the dip with oil. Serve the dip with the pita wedges.

Note: This sauce can be kept in the refrigerator for up to 2 days.

appeteasers, snacks, and dippidy-do dips

creamy spinach-artichoke dip

People love this American restaurant classic, but it's usually packed with calories. I took on the challenge and came up with a healthier version that's even more delicious. I promise you won't miss the cream or mayonnaise in this recipe, let alone the calories!

MAKES 4 TO 6 SERVINGS

cooking spray

2 tablespoons olive oil

1 medium yellow onion, finely diced

1 garlic clove, minced

1 10-ounce box of chopped frozen spinach, thawed and squeezed dry

1 10-ounce can artichoke hearts, drained and chopped

2 teaspoons Worcestershire sauce

1 to 2 dashes of Tabasco

½ cup crumbled reduced-fat feta

½ cup low-fat sour cream

salt

freshly ground pepper

3 tablespoons freshly grated Parmesan cheese

Pumpernickel or rye toast, for serving

1. Preheat the oven to 375°F. Lightly spray an 8-inch-square baking pan with cooking spray.

2. Heat the olive oil in a medium skillet over medium heat. Add the onion and cook, stirring often, just until beginning to soften, about 1 minute. Stir in the garlic. Add the spinach, artichokes, Worcestershire sauce, and Tabasco. Cook, stirring often, just until heated through, about 1 minute. Remove from the heat and stir in the feta and sour cream. Season with salt and pepper. Spread in the baking dish and sprinkle with the Parmesan on top.

3. Bake until the dip is bubbling and lightly browned, 20 to 25 minutes. Serve hot, with the toast.

watermelon tropical fiesta salsa

Since watermelon and cucumbers are botanically related, I often use them together in unexpected ways. In this salsa, watermelon and mango take the place of tomatoes. Serve this light and summery salsa with baked tortilla chips or as an accompaniment to grilled fish or chicken.

1 cup (¼-inch dice) seedless watermelon, peeled and diced

1 cup (¼-inch dice) mango, peeled, pitted, and diced

1 cup (¼-inch dice) cucumber, peeled, seeded, and diced

1 jalapeño, seeded and ribbed, minced

¼ cup fresh lime juice

2 tablespoons fresh cilantro, finely chopped

1 tablespoon fresh flat-leaf Italian parsley leaves, finely chopped

kosher salt

freshly ground black pepper

Mix the watermelon, mango, cucumber, and jalapeño in a medium bowl. Stir in the lime juice, cilantro, and parsley. Season with salt and pepper. Refrigerate for at least 30 minutes and up to 1 hour. Serve chilled.

Indulge!

plantain fritters *(arañitas)* with avocadolicious dip

Unlike traditional fried plantains—*tostones*—that are sliced, fried, mashed, then fried again, these fritters are grated and fried once, making them similar to potato pancakes. In Spanish, *arañitas* mean "little spiders," and this recipe gets its name from the shredded plantains, which crawl or spread out when fried. These are so good that they deserve their own Avocadolicious Dip.

MAKES 4 SERVINGS

canola oil for frying

4 garlic cloves

kosher salt

3 green plantains, peeled and shredded on the large holes of a box grater

freshly ground black pepper

¼ cup chopped fresh cilantro

1. Heat 2 inches of oil to 350°F in a heavy skillet or deep pot over medium-high heat. Line a plate with paper towels and set aside.

2. While the oil heats, place the garlic cloves on a cutting board. Slice the cloves in half lengthwise and then smash with the side of a chef's knife. Sprinkle a pinch of salt over the garlic and chop and smear the garlic against the cutting board until it makes a paste.

3. Place the grated plantains, garlic paste, and pepper in a large bowl and mix until combined. Using a spoon, scoop out about a tablespoon of the mixture and press it flat with the back of another spoon. Gently slide it in the hot oil, adding enough fritters to fill the pan without crowding. Fry until golden, for 4 to 5 minutes on each side. (If the fritters get too dark too quickly, lower the temperature.) Using a slotted spoon or frying spider, transfer the fritters to the paper towels to drain. Sprinkle with salt and cilantro and serve warm.

CHICA TIP

! Plantains—*plátanos* in Spanish—are a member of the banana family, but larger and with much thicker skins, making them difficult to peel. When unripe, the peel is green; when ripe, black but not rotten. To peel green plantains, put them in a shallow dish with enough hot tap water to cover. Soak for 5 minutes. Remove from the water. Slice off both ends, then make four or five vertical slices on the plantain without cutting into the flesh. Remove the peel with your hands.

appeteasers, snacks, and dippidy-do dips

avocadolicious dip

This creamy blend of avocado, mayonnaise, and cream cheese makes a smooth dip that goes well with plantain fritters. You can also add a dollop to a bowl of soup or use it as a spread on sandwiches.

MAKES 4 SERVINGS

1 Hass avocado, halved, seeded, and peeled

⅓ cup mayonnaise (regular or light)

⅓ cup cream cheese

2 scallions, white and light green part only, chopped

1 jalapeño, seeded and finely chopped

2 tablespoons fresh lime juice

kosher salt

freshly ground black pepper

Plantain Fritters (page 61)

Process the avocado, mayonnaise, cream cheese, scallions, jalapeño, and lime juice in a food processor or blender until the mixture is smooth, about 1 minute. Season with salt and pepper. Serve immediately.

roasted tomato sopa

soups
for the soul

When I was growing up, lunch, our main meal of the day, always started with a bowl of comforting soup. My mom told us that a serving of warm soup would fill us up and keep us from overeating. So true. I also find that sipping a cup of Lime and Escarole Soup or Roasted Tomato Sopa tames those in-between meal cravings.

To thicken soups without using cream, flour, or potatoes, I double up on the vegetables, and once they are cooked, I puree them in a blender. For a chunky soup, puree one or two cups of the cooked vegetables. When the puree is added back to the pot, the soup will be thicker and more of the vegetables' flavors will come through. For velvety soups, puree the entire mixture.

Cold soups and those that contain seafood such as *Sopa de Paella* and *Aguadito* don't freeze well. All of my other soups can be frozen and reheated without any changes to their flavors and textures. Double the recipes and freeze the soup in individual-serving-size containers. You'll always have a homemade meal on hand.

Finally, soups like Cabbage, Chayote, and Chicken Soup and *Sopa de Paella* are hearty one-pot meals. Add a salad and you have dinner.

cabbage, chayote, and chicken soup

While I love a bowl of nourishing chicken soup, I'm not a big fan when noodles or rice is added. I prefer mine with pieces of chicken and lots of vegetables. Just before serving, I add some sliced avocado and a squeeze of lime juice to brighten the flavors.

MAKES 6 TO 8 SERVINGS

1 tablespoon olive oil

½ medium yellow onion, chopped

2 cups packed green cabbage, shredded

2 tablespoons fresh cilantro, finely chopped

2 garlic cloves, minced

1 teaspoon dried oregano

1 teaspoon Delicioso Adobo Seasoning (page 8)

6 cups low-sodium chicken broth

2 chayotes, peeled and cut into 1-inch pieces

1 pound chicken tenders, cut in half crosswise

1 Hass avocado, halved, pitted, peeled, and sliced

lime wedges, for serving

1. Heat the oil in a large saucepan over medium heat. Add the onion and cook, stirring occasionally, until lightly browned, about 5 minutes. Add the cabbage, cilantro, garlic, oregano, and adobo and cook until the cabbage begins to soften, about 4 minutes. Add the broth and chayote. Reduce the heat to medium-low and simmer about 15 minutes. Add the chicken tenders and simmer the soup for another 15 minutes.

2. Ladle the soup into soup bowls. Serve hot, accompanied by the avocado slices and the lime wedges.

CHICA TIP

! When peeling the chayote, make sure to wear gloves because it can be really slippery and the liquid can peel the skin off your hands.

roasted tomato sopa

Tomato soup is a classic that many remember from childhood. I decided that grown-ups deserve a new version with roasted tomatoes and onions, herbs, and some ground cumin.

cooking spray

2 pounds tomatoes, cut in halves crosswise

2 medium yellow onions, cut lengthwise into quarters

4 tablespoons olive oil

kosher salt

freshly ground black pepper

6 garlic cloves, minced

1 teaspoon fresh oregano leaves, finely chopped

1 teaspoon fresh thyme leaves, finely chopped

2 cups low-sodium chicken or vegetable broth

2 teaspoons light or dark brown sugar

1 teaspoon Worcestershire sauce

¼ teaspoon ground cumin

½ cup nonfat Greek-style yogurt

2 tablespoons slivered almonds

2 tablespoons freshly grated Parmesan cheese

2 tablespoons fresh cilantro, finely chopped

CHICA TIP

! Keep a package of slivered almonds in the freezer to use as a soup garnish instead of bread croutons.

1. Preheat the oven to 400°F.

2. Spray 2 large glass or ceramic baking dishes with cooking spray. Arrange the vegetables, cut sides up, in the baking dishes and brush with 2 tablespoons of oil. Season with salt and pepper. Roast until the onions are softened and browned, about 45 minutes. Let cool. Transfer the tomatoes and onions to a blender or food processor and puree in 2 batches.

3. Heat the remaining 2 tablespoons of oil in a medium saucepan over medium heat. Add the garlic and cook, stirring often, until golden. Stir in the oregano and thyme. If the oil is absorbed by the garlic and herbs, add 2 to 4 tablespoons of broth (don't add more oil) and cook over medium-low heat until the broth evaporates (2 to 3 minutes).

4. Add the pureed vegetables with the remaining chicken broth, brown sugar, Worcestershire sauce, and cumin. Season with salt and pepper. Bring to a simmer and cook for 8 minutes.

5. Ladle the soup into bowls. Top each serving with a dollop of yogurt; then sprinkle with almonds, Parmesan, and cilantro. Serve hot.

quinoa vegetable soup

While quinoa has become more popular in recent years, my family ate it often because it was a staple on the table of my Bolivian grandfather, Eduardo Ybarnegaray, when he was growing up.

MAKES 6 SERVINGS

2 tablespoons olive oil

3 medium carrots, cut into ½-inch dice

3 scallions, white and pale green parts only, cut into 1-inch lengths

1 medium zucchini, halved and cut into 1-inch pieces

¼ cup fresh flat-leaf parsley, finely chopped, plus more for garnish

2 small garlic cloves, finely minced

1 teaspoon oregano leaves, chopped

½ teaspoon ground cumin

4 cups low-sodium chicken or vegetable broth

2 14-ounce cans roasted tomatoes with juices, chopped

2 cups water

1 cup quinoa, rinsed in a sieve and drained well

1 bay leaf

kosher salt

freshly ground black pepper

2 Hass avocados, halved, pitted, peeled, and sliced

1. Heat the oil in a large saucepan over medium heat. Add the carrots, scallions, and zucchini and cook, stirring often, until the zucchini softens, about 4 minutes. Add the parsley, garlic, oregano, and cumin and stir well. Add the broth, tomatoes with their juices, water, quinoa, and bay leaf and bring to a boil. Reduce the heat to medium-low and simmer until the quinoa is tender, about 20 minutes. Season with salt and pepper.

2. Divide the avocado evenly among soup bowls. Ladle the soup into the bowls, sprinkle with parsley, and serve hot.

garlic soup

In Spain, garlic soup originally was a peasant dish of fried garlic and bread in water. Through the years, other ingredients—a sprinkle of cayenne and a few saffron strands for color and chicken broth for richness—were added. The garlic mellows as it simmers and softens. The final flourish is a poached egg nestled on top; when you cut into it, the runny yolk oozes into the broth, making it extra luxurious.

MAKES 4 SERVINGS

6 tablespoons olive oil

12 garlic cloves, peeled

4 1-inch-thick diagonal slices from a whole-wheat baguette

4 cups low-sodium chicken broth

1 teaspoon sweet paprika, preferably Spanish

kosher salt

freshly ground black pepper

4 large eggs

fresh flat-leaf parsley leaves, chopped, for garnish

1. Heat the oil in a large saucepan over medium-high heat until very hot but not smoking. Add the garlic and fry until golden brown, about 1 minute. Using a slotted spoon, transfer the garlic to a plate. Add the bread, cut side down, and cook, turning once, until golden brown, about 3 minutes. Transfer to the plate with the garlic.

2. Return the garlic to the saucepan. Add the broth and paprika, bring to a boil, and cook to blend the flavors, about 5 minutes. Season with salt and pepper. Reduce the heat to medium-low so the broth is simmering. Crack an egg into a small bowl; then slip the egg into the simmering broth. Repeat with the remaining eggs. Simmer until the whites are set (you are basically poaching the eggs in the broth), about 4 minutes.

3. Ladle the soup into 4 soup bowls. Using a slotted spoon, transfer a poached egg to each bowl. Top with a fried bread slice. Sprinkle with parsley and serve hot.

roasted red peppers and lentil soup

I like my lentil soup with plenty of vegetables, including roasted red peppers from a jar, and seasonings. Since lentils don't require soaking, this soup can be on the table in well under an hour. It's even better the next day.

1 tablespoon olive oil

½ cup yellow onion, chopped

¼ cup celery, chopped

¼ cup carrots, chopped

1 cup dried lentils, rinsed and drained

½ cup roasted and jarred red peppers, chopped

6 cups low-sodium chicken or vegetable broth

¼ cup fresh flat-leaf parsley leaves, chopped

½ teaspoon fresh oregano leaves, chopped

⅛ teaspoon ground cumin

1 teaspoon red wine vinegar

kosher salt

freshly ground black pepper

1. Heat the oil in a large saucepan over medium heat. Add the onion, celery, and carrots and cook, stirring often, until the onions are translucent, about 3 minutes.

2. Add the lentils, red peppers, broth, 1 tablespoon of parsley, oregano, and cumin. Bring to a boil. Reduce the heat to medium-low and simmer until the lentils are tender, about 35 minutes. Stir in the vinegar. Let cool slightly.

3. In batches, puree the soup in a blender with the blender lid ajar, and pour into a clean pot. (Or puree the soup directly in the cooking pot with an immersion blender.) Reheat the soup. Season with salt and pepper. Ladle into bowls and sprinkle each serving with the remaining parsley. Serve hot.

lime and escarole soup

The tanginess of lime pairs unexpectedly well with the rustic bitterness of escarole in this brothy Mexican chicken soup. A kick of jalapeño and garlic add just enough oomph; cilantro pumps up the lime's citrusy aroma, while gritty cloves and cumin haunt the final dish, adding sweet and savory notes to every spoonful. For a dish that's a bit heartier, add a poached egg or some shredded chicken to each bowl before serving.

MAKES 4 SERVINGS

1 tablespoon olive oil

2 small yellow onions, each cut into quarters

2 jalapeños, halved and seeded

8 garlic cloves, crushed under a knife and peeled

¼ teaspoon ground cumin

4 whole cloves

4 cups low-sodium chicken broth

1 head escarole, torn or chopped into bite-size pieces, well rinsed (about 8 cups, loosely packed)

2 tablespoons fresh lime juice

¼ teaspoon Tabasco (optional)

kosher salt

½ cup fresh cilantro, coarsely chopped

3 tablespoons fresh lime zest

1. Heat the oil in a large saucepan over medium-high heat. Add the onions, jalapeños, garlic, cumin, and cloves and cook, stirring often, until the onions are translucent but not browned, about 4 minutes. Add the broth and bring to a boil. Cover, reduce the heat, and simmer until the broth is fragrant, about 20 minutes. Strain the broth through a wire sieve over a large heatproof bowl. Discard the solids in the sieve.

2. Return the broth to the saucepan and bring to a gentle simmer over medium heat. Add the escarole, lime juice, and Tabasco, if using. Season with the salt. Cover and simmer until the escarole is tender, about 8 to 10 minutes. Remove from the heat. Stir in the cilantro and lime zest.

3. Ladle the soup into bowls and serve hot.

sweet potato and chicken soup

This is how my mom made chicken soup for me—rich with potatoes, yuca, other vegetables, and plenty of seasonings. I could consume bowls and bowls of her soup.

MAKES 6 TO 8 SERVINGS

2 tablespoons olive oil

1 4-pound chicken, preferably organic, quartered

1 large yellow onion, cut into ½-inch dice

2 large carrots, cut into ½-inch dice

4 medium celery stalks, cut into ½-inch dice

1 medium red bell pepper, cored, seeded, ribbed, and cut into ½-inch dice

1 medium yuca, peeled and cut into ½-inch cubes, or use frozen yuca

1 large sweet potato, peeled and cut into ½-inch cubes

⅛ teaspoon ground cumin

⅛ teaspoon ground achiote

8 cups water or low-sodium chicken or vegetable broth

1 fresh cilantro, chopped

1 jalapeño, seeded and minced, or a few shakes of Tabasco (optional)

3 garlic cloves, minced

1 tablespoon fresh oregano leaves, chopped

kosher salt

freshly ground black pepper

lime halves, for serving

1. Heat 1 tablespoon of oil in a large Dutch oven over medium heat until hot but not smoking. In batches, add the chicken, skin side down, and cook, turning occasionally, until lightly browned, about 5 minutes. Transfer to a plate.

2. Add the remaining oil to the Dutch oven and heat. Add the onion, carrot, celery, red pepper, yuca, sweet potato, cumin, and achiote. Cook, stirring occasionally, until the onions are translucent, about 8 minutes.

3. Return the chicken to the Dutch oven. Add the water, half of the cilantro, the jalapeño, garlic, and oregano. Bring to a boil; then reduce heat to low and simmer until the chicken is tender, 35 to 40 minutes. Season with salt and pepper.

4. Using tongs, transfer the chicken to a chopping board. Let cool slightly; then discard the skin and bones and shred the meat. Stir the chicken back into the soup.

5. For each serving, squeeze a lime half into a soup bowl. Ladle in the soup, sprinkle with some of the remaining cilantro, and serve hot.

CHICA TIP

Yuca, also known as cassava or manioc, is a starchy tuber that looks similar to a sweet potato. A staple in Latin and African cooking, yuca can be boiled, steamed, ground into flour for baking, or used as a thickener (tapioca comes from the yuca root). Look for firm, fresh or peeled, frozen yuca at the market. Like for potatoes, store fresh yuca in a cool, dry place.

venezuelan black bean soup

Friends in Caracas taught me how to make *caraotas negras*, black beans cooked Venezuelan style. Pair this with a salad, some steamed vegetables, and some brown rice for a satisfying meal. I'm always amazed how a simple ingredient like beans can taste when put in the hands of different cooks.

1 tablespoon olive oil

1 medium yellow onion, chopped

1 medium green bell pepper, cored, ribbed, seeded, and chopped

4 scallions, white and green parts, chopped

1 garlic clove, minced

1 tablespoon ground cumin

2 15-ounce cans black beans; do not drain and rinse

2 cups low-sodium chicken broth

¼ cup plus 2 tablespoons fresh cilantro, chopped

1 tablespoon Scotch (optional)

kosher salt

freshly ground black pepper

extra-virgin olive oil, for serving (optional)

1. Heat the oil in a large saucepan over medium heat. Add the onion, green pepper, scallions, garlic, and cumin and cook, stirring occasionally, until the vegetables are tender, about 8 minutes. Add the beans with their liquid, the broth, ¼ cup of cilantro, and the whiskey, if using, and bring to a boil. Reduce the heat to medium-low and simmer, stirring occasionally, until the flavors are blended, about 10 minutes. Season with salt and pepper.

2. Ladle the soup into soup bowls. Sprinkle each with the remaining cilantro, and drizzle with olive oil, if desired. Serve hot.

chilled cucumber-coconut soup

When it's just too hot to even think about turning on the oven, turn to this cooling soup. Crisp cucumbers are blended with light coconut milk, rich Greek yogurt, a bit of onion, and fresh mint leaves for an easy-on-the-cook summer soup.

MAKES 4 SERVINGS

3 cucumbers

⅓ cup red onion, chopped

1½ cups light unsweetened coconut milk

¼ cup plus 2 tablespoons nonfat or reduced-fat Greek yogurt

2 tablespoons fresh lime juice

5 mint leaves

½ teaspoon ground turmeric

½ teaspoon freshly ground white pepper

kosher salt

1. Peel the cucumbers. Cut each in half lengthwise and scoop out the seeds with the tip of a spoon. Coarsely chop the cucumbers.

2. Puree the cucumbers, red onion, coconut milk, 2 tablespoons of yogurt, lime juice, mint, turmeric, white pepper, and salt in a food processor. (Or combine the ingredients in a bowl, puree in batches in a blender, and pour into another bowl.) Cover with plastic wrap and refrigerate until chilled, at least 2 hours and up to 8 hours.

3. Ladle the soup into soup bowls. Top each with a dollop of the remaining yogurt and serve chilled.

blueberry-watermelon gazpacho

Who needs tomatoes to make gazpacho? This slightly sweet, slightly spicy blend of blueberries, watermelon, and bell peppers is a change from the traditional vegetable version and gives you a peek into how I like to play with different flavors and ingredients. A bowl of this refreshing no-cook soup is perfect on a hot summer's night when all of the ingredients are in season.

MAKES 4 SERVINGS

5 cups (¼-inch dice) seedless watermelon

1½ cups fresh blueberries

1 medium cucumber, peeled, halved lengthwise, seeded, and cut into ¼-inch dice

⅓ cup red wine vinegar or fruit-infused vinegar

½ cup chopped fresh cilantro, basil, or mint leaves

½ medium red onion, chopped

½ medium yellow bell pepper, cored, seeded, ribbed, and chopped

1 small jalapeño, seeded and minced

kosher salt

freshly ground black pepper (optional)

1 ripe Hass avocado, halved, seeded, peeled, and cut into slivers

1. Puree 4 cups of the watermelon, the blueberries, half of the cucumber, and the vinegar in a blender or food processor. Add all but 1 tablespoon of cilantro with the onion, yellow pepper, and as much jalapeño as you like, and process until finely chopped. Pour into a bowl and stir in the remaining watermelon and cucumber. Season with salt and pepper, if desired.

2. Cover and refrigerate until chilled, at least 2 hours and up to 5 hours.

3. Ladle into bowls and sprinkle with avocado and remaining cilantro. Serve chilled.

CHICA TIP

! At your next party, pass martini or shot glasses filled with chilled or room temperature soups. Your guests will love them.

gazpacho

The city of Seville in Andalucía, the southernmost region in Spain, is said to be the birthplace of this popular chilled soup that requires no cooking. Some people like a chunky gazpacho, but I prefer mine pureed and strained for a smooth, silky soup. It's your call; puree the soup as much or as little as you wish. Serve the soup chilled, but not too cold, or the flavors will be dull. You can heat the gazpacho as well. Pass a tray of gazpacho in shot glasses at your next party.

MAKES 4 TO 6 SERVINGS

4 ripe large tomatoes

3 1-inch-thick slices French baguette, crusts removed

2 tablespoons sherry wine vinegar

2 tablespoons water

2 garlic cloves, minced

1 cucumber, peeled, seeded, and cut into ¼-inch dice

½ small green bell pepper, cored, seeded, ribbed, and cut into ¼-inch dice

2 tablespoons extra-virgin olive oil

kosher salt

freshly ground black pepper

2 tablespoons fresh chives, finely chopped, for garnish

1. Fill two-thirds of a medium saucepan with water and bring to a boil over high heat. Using a paring knife, score a small X on the smooth end of each tomato. Remove the saucepan from the heat. Add the tomatoes and let stand until the skins soften. Using a slotted spoon, transfer the tomatoes to a colander and let cool until easy to handle. Peel off the tomato skins. Cut each tomato in half and poke out the seeds with your forefinger. Coarsely chop the tomatoes.

2. Combine the baguette slices, vinegar, water, and garlic together in a small bowl. Let stand until the bread is mushy, about 10 minutes. This mixture acts as a thickener and flavors the soup with garlic, too.

3. Place three-quarters each of the cucumber and green pepper in a medium bowl, and add the tomatoes and the bread mixture. Combine the remaining cucumber and green pepper in a small bowl, cover, and refrigerate for garnishing the soup. Puree the tomato mixture in a food processor. With the processor running, add the oil. For a smoother soup, add a tablespoon or so of water. (Or, in batches, puree in a blender, and return to the bowl, adding the oil to the final batch.) Season with salt and pepper. Strain the soup through a medium wire sieve into another bowl. Cover with plastic wrap and refrigerate to blend the flavors, at least 1 hour and up to 8 hours. Let stand at room temperature for 30 minutes before serving so the soup isn't too cold.

4. Ladle the soup into chilled soup bowls. Top each with some of the chopped cucumber and green peppers, and sprinkle with chives.

CHICA TIP

! Chill shot glasses on a tray in the freezer for twenty to thirty minutes before filling them with the cold soup. The frosted mini glasses will be a hit—and a conversation starter—at your summer parties and barbecues.

sopa de paella

I love paella. I love soups. So I decided to play with all the bold flavors and classic ingredients of paella, Spain's most famous dish, and make a comforting soup with *mucho sabor* and many ingredients. White meat chicken, shrimp, just a hint of chorizo, and some brown rice are all simmered together in a colorful saffron-scented broth for an all-in-one dish. Everything you need—protein, starch, and vegetables—can be found in this healthy soup.

MAKES 6 SERVINGS

1 tablespoon olive oil

1 medium yellow onion, finely chopped

1 medium green bell pepper, cored, seeded, ribbed, and finely chopped

3 plum tomatoes, seeded and diced

1 serrano chile, seeded and minced

2 garlic cloves, minced

6 cups low-sodium chicken broth

½ cup brown rice

¼ teaspoon crushed saffron threads

2 boneless, skinless chicken breast halves (about 12 ounces), cut into thin strips

½ pound medium shrimp, peeled and deveined

1 ounce cured Spanish chorizo sausage, thinly sliced

1 cup thawed frozen or cooked fresh peas

kosher salt

freshly ground black pepper

1. Heat the oil in a large Dutch oven over medium-high heat. Add the onion and green pepper and cook, stirring occasionally, until the vegetables are very tender, 8 to 10 minutes. Add the tomatoes, chile, and garlic and cook, stirring occasionally, until the tomatoes are soft, about 6 minutes.

2. Stir in the broth, rice, and saffron and bring to a boil. Reduce the heat to medium low and partially cover the Dutch oven. Simmer until the brown rice is tender, about 40 minutes. Add the chicken, shrimp, chorizo, and peas and cook until the chicken and shrimp are opaque, about 4 minutes. Season with salt and pepper. Ladle into bowls and serve hot.

butternut squash–coconut soup

While butternut squash soup is a traditional first course at many autumn meals, I find that most versions are bland and could use a burst of bold flavors. I start with coconut milk to take this classic to another level. Cinnamon and nutmeg balanced by the zip of fresh ginger and serrano chile make this one a standout. You'll never make butternut squash soup any other way.

2 teaspoons olive oil

3 large shallots, thinly sliced (⅓ cup)

¼ cup fresh ginger, peeled and chopped

2 garlic cloves, minced

1 serrano chile pepper, seeded and chopped

1 tablespoon plus 1 teaspoon light brown sugar

4 cups low-sodium vegetable broth

1½ pounds butternut squash, peeled and cut into chunks

2 3-inch cinnamon sticks

½ teaspoon salt

¼ teaspoon freshly grated nutmeg

½ cup light coconut milk

3 tablespoons fresh cilantro, chopped

1 tablespoon freshly grated lime zest

1 tablespoon fresh lime juice

1. Heat the oil in a Dutch oven over medium heat. Add the shallots, ginger, garlic, and chile. Cook, stirring constantly, until fragrant, 2 to 3 minutes. Add the sugar and cook, stirring, until the shallots just begin to brown, about 2 minutes. Stir in the broth, squash, cinnamon sticks, salt, and nutmeg and bring to a boil. Reduce the heat to medium low and simmer, partially covered, until the squash is fork-tender, about 20 minutes. Remove from heat and let cool for 10 minutes. Remove and discard the cinnamon sticks.

2. In batches, puree the soup in a food processor or blender. Return the soup to the saucepan (or use a handheld immersion blender to puree the soup in the pot). Stir in the coconut milk, cilantro, lime zest, and juice, and heat through. Ladle into bowls and serve hot.

CHICA TIP

Peeled and cubed butternut squash is now available in supermarkets, so making this soup is a snap!

portobello, leek, and sherry soup

Whatever happened to serving warm soup as a first course? Soups come together quickly and can, for the most part, be made ahead and reheated. My creamy portobello soup—made without cream—fits the bill. My guests are always thrilled when they sit down to bowls of soup. The richness and intense flavors come from the leeks and mushrooms, which are sautéed in a bit of butter before they are pureed. A splash of dry sherry adds just a bit of nuttiness to the soup.

MAKES 4 TO 6 SERVINGS

2 tablespoons unsalted butter

2 medium leeks, white and pale green parts only, thinly sliced and rinsed well

6 portobello mushroom caps, about 3 ounces each, chopped

2 tablespoons all-purpose flour

4 cups low-sodium chicken broth

4 cups water

¼ cup dry sherry or Madeira

kosher salt

freshly ground white pepper

½ cup nonfat Greek yogurt, for serving

3 tablespoons fresh flat-leaf parsley, finely chopped, for serving

1 whole-wheat baguette, sliced

1. Melt the butter in a large saucepan over medium-high heat until lightly browned. Browning brings out the flavor of the butter, but be careful that you don't cook it beyond a light hazelnut color. Add the leeks and cook, stirring often, until the leeks are softened, about 2 minutes. Add the mushrooms, stirring occasionally until the mushrooms are tender and any liquid is evaporated, about 10 minutes. Sprinkle with the flour and cook, stirring almost constantly, to cook the flour without browning, for 2 minutes.

2. Stir in the broth, water, and sherry and bring to a boil. Reduce the heat and simmer, stirring occasionally, until the flavors are blended and the soup is slightly thickened, about 10 minutes. Season with salt and white pepper to taste. In batches, puree the soup in a blender with the blender lid ajar. Transfer to a clean saucepan. Reheat the soup.

3. Ladle the soup into soup bowls. Top each with a dollop of yogurt, sprinkle with parsley, and serve hot with slices of baguette.

peruvian seafood soup
(*aguadito de mariscos*)

This is a traditional soup from Peru chock-full of clams, calamari, and shrimp, with generous amounts of bright green cilantro and the sweet heat of brick red *ají panca* chile. I often serve this seafood soup when entertaining. While this may seem like a lot, I promise you there won't be any leftovers.

MAKES 10 SERVINGS

1 cup packed fresh cilantro

¼ cup water

2 tablespoons canola oil

1 medium yellow onion, diced

4 garlic cloves, minced

1 teaspoon sweet paprika

1 tablespoon *ají panca* chile paste or pasilla chile paste

3 quarts fish stock

salt

freshly ground pepper

2 clusters snow crab legs

20 littleneck clams, scrubbed and rinsed

8 ounces bay scallops

1 pound medium shrimp, peeled and deveined

1 pound cleaned calamari, cut into ¼-inch rings

1 cup fresh or frozen green peas

¾ cup long-grain rice

1 cup (½-inch dice) butternut squash, peeled and seeded

2 scallions, white and pale green parts only, thinly sliced, for serving

lime wedges, for serving

1. Puree the cilantro and water together in a blender or food processor. Set aside, but use within 15 minutes or it will discolor.

2. Heat the oil in a stockpot over medium-high heat. Add the onion and garlic and cook, stirring often, until softened, about 2 minutes. Stir in the cilantro puree and the paprika and cook until slightly thickened, about 2 minutes. Add the *ají panca* paste and stock and season with salt and pepper. Cover and simmer to blend the flavors, about 10 minutes.

3. Stir in the crab clusters, clams, scallops, shrimp, calamari, peas, rice, and squash. Cover and simmer until the squash is very tender, about 30 minutes.

4. Ladle into soup bowls. Sprinkle each serving with scallions and serve with the lime wedges to squeeze the juice into the soup.

carrot, orange, and ginger soup

Carrot soup is too often bland and boring, but with the addition of orange zest and juice and some fresh, spicy ginger, my version is bright and brilliant. Serve hot before dinner in the autumn and winter months or chilled in margarita glasses as a first course during the summer.

MAKES 4 TO 6 SERVINGS

1 tablespoon olive oil

1 tablespoon unsalted butter

2 leeks, white and pale green parts only, sliced and well rinsed

4 cups low-sodium chicken broth

6 medium carrots, peeled and chopped

1 pound medium red potatoes, peeled and cut into 1-inch chunks

freshly grated zest of 1 orange

½ cup fresh orange juice

1 tablespoon fresh ginger, peeled and grated

salt

freshly ground white pepper

orange slices, for garnish

fresh mint leaves, for garnish

1. Heat the oil and butter in a Dutch oven over medium-high heat. Add the leeks and cook, stirring occasionally, until tender, about 5 minutes. Add the broth, carrots, potatoes, orange zest, juice, and ginger. Season with salt and pepper. Bring to a boil. Reduce the heat to medium low and simmer, stirring occasionally until the potatoes and carrots are very tender, about 25 minutes.

2. In batches, puree the soup in a blender with the blender lid ajar, and pour into a clean pot (or puree the soup directly in the cooking pot with an immersion blender). Reheat the soup. Ladle into bowls and top each serving with an orange slice and some mint leaves. Serve hot.

CHICA TIP

> **To save my knuckles, I use a microplane rasp to grate ingredients like the zests of citrus fruits, ginger, and scallions.**

soups for the soul

power-up spinach soup

Spinach is a super food with a long list of benefits. It's low in calories and high in phytonutrients, vitamins, and minerals. Spinach, like other dark leafy greens, contains folate, which can actually help improve your mood! I add ginger, onion, and clove, which all take the "blah" out of this good-for-you soup.

MAKES 6 SERVINGS

2 tablespoons olive oil

1½ yellow onions, chopped

2 garlic cloves, finely chopped

1 2-inch piece fresh ginger root, peeled and grated

3 medium potatoes, peeled and thinly sliced

6 cups chicken broth, homemade or canned low-sodium broth

10 ounces washed spinach leaves (about 6 cups), and a few extra leaves set aside and finely shredded for garnishing

1 teaspoon salt

fresh black pepper

1 lemon, zested, plus 2 tablespoons lemon juice

1. Heat the oil in a large pot over medium-high heat for 1 minute. Add the onion, garlic, and ginger and cook until soft and golden, about 5 minutes, stirring often. Add the potatoes and cook until they are just starting to brown around the edges, about 5 minutes. Add the chicken stock and simmer for 15 minutes.

2. Stir in the spinach leaves, making sure that they are all submerged, and cook until they are wilted, about 2 minutes. Season the soup with salt, pepper, and lemon juice and turn off the heat.

3. Transfer some of the soup to a blender and puree. (When blending hot liquids, fill the blender less than halfway full, place the lid askew and pulse the liquid at first to release some heat. Otherwise your blender top could pop!) Transfer the soup to a clean pot and repeat with the remaining soup.

4. Reheat the soup and serve sprinkled with the shredded spinach leaves and some lemon zest.

Indulge!

mexican corn soup

By using less bacon and replacing the heavy cream with Greek yogurt, this classic comfort soup becomes lighter but retains its authentic flavors. Rich and creamy, this filling and warming soup is unbeatable on a chilly day when I deserve a treat.

MAKES 4 TO 6 SERVINGS

4 ears fresh corn or 3 cups frozen corn kernels, thawed

2 medium tomatoes, coarsely chopped

1 quart low-sodium chicken broth

½ teaspoon dried oregano

4 slices thick-cut bacon

½ medium yellow onion, chopped (about 1 cup)

2 garlic cloves, minced

kosher salt

freshly ground black pepper

3 tablespoons fresh flat-leaf parsley, chopped

½ cup heavy cream (see *Chica Tip* below)

½ cup *queso fresco*, fresh farmer's cheese, feta, or sour cream (optional)

tortilla chips, for serving

CHICA TIP

! For a lighter touch, use Greek-style nonfat plain yogurt in place of heavy cream.

1. If using fresh corn, scrape the kernels from the cobs using a small sharp knife or a spoon. Puree half of the corn kernels in a blender with the tomatoes, 2 cups of broth, and the oregano.

2. Cook the bacon in a large saucepan over medium heat, turning once, until brown and crisp, about 10 minutes. Transfer the bacon to a paper towel–lined plate to drain, leaving the fat in the saucepan.

3. Add the onion to the saucepan and cook, stirring frequently, until the onion is soft and translucent, about 3 minutes. Add the garlic and stir until fragrant, about 1 minute.

4. Add the tomato-corn puree to the saucepan with the remaining 2 cups of broth. Bring to a simmer over medium-low heat. Add the reserved corn kernels and cook until thickened, stirring occasionally and skimming off any foam from the surface, about 20 minutes. Season with salt and pepper.

5. Crumble the cooled bacon. Mix in half of the parsley and the cream, if using, and heat through. Ladle into bowls and top each serving with bacon, *queso fresco*, tortilla chips, and the remaining parsley.

farmers' market roasted vegetable
salad in avocado cups

going green: salads

5

I'm a salad girl. They are must-haves with most meals. It's as if my body asks—or begs—me for salad. I love being adventurous with salads and dressings and include ingredients often not found in salads. This way, I never get bored.

When I say "salads," I mean big, hearty salads layered with all kinds of textures and ingredients from pale frisée to leafy, dark green spinach and watercress; a colorful array of roasted vegetables like zucchini, eggplant and fennel; and plenty of my favorite fruits like avocados and mangoes. And when I want to make a meal out of them, I just top them with grilled and sliced chicken or steak or some shrimp.

I love making my own salad dressings. They're so easy! Just whisk the ingredients together in a bowl or shake them in a lidded jar. And you know exactly what's going into your dressings. High-fat dressing can make any salad as high caloric as a fully decked burger. You'll never find bottled salad dressings in my fridge—I can't stand them! Who needs all the sugar and preservatives when you can easily make your own?

As with all cooking, your food will be only as good as the ingredients you start with. Especially for salads, the oils, vinegars, and seasonings you choose make a big difference. Salad time is the ideal time to use that special extra-virgin olive oil or that mango-infused vinegar purchased at a farmers' market. You don't need much, but top-notch condiments do make all the difference.

For the most part, salt should be added to the dressing once all the other ingredients are combined. Taste a bit of the dressing and add salt as needed. When it comes to cooking or blanching vegetables, I use kosher salt. For finishing dishes, however, I prefer pink salt for its pure flavor. You may like the flavor of Maldon or some other sea salt. That's why I simply call for salt, leaving the type up to you!

Salads make a satisfying meal for this chica. They'll do the same for you.

jicama slaw

Jicama has the crunchiness of celery, the starchiness of potatoes, and the sweetness of apples. Once the brown skin is peeled away, I grate the white interior on a box grater and use it in place of cabbage for a Latin-inspired slaw. Fresh lime juice—no mayonnaise—is the only dressing you need, making this your go-to healthy salad when you're looking for something light. Spoon some of this slaw on turkey sandwiches or grilled turkey burgers.

MAKES 6 SERVINGS

1 pound jicama (about 1 medium)

1 cup fresh cilantro, chopped

½ cup green bell pepper, diced

½ cup red bell pepper, diced

½ cup red onion, diced

1 teaspoon garlic, minced

3 tablespoons fresh lime juice

kosher salt

freshly ground black pepper

1. Peel the jicama using a vegetable peeler; discard the peel. Grate the jicama using the largest holes on a box grater.

2. Combine the jicama with the cilantro, green pepper, red pepper, onion, and garlic. Drizzle with lime juice and toss to combine. Season with salt and pepper, to taste. Cover and refrigerate until chilled, at least 1 hour. Serve chilled.

CHICA TIP

Can't find jicama? No problem. Use crisp apples or Asian pears instead.

watercress and chayote salad with mango vinaigrette

If you're unfamiliar with chayote, this crunchy salad will win you over. Like its family members zucchini and cucumbers, chayote can be eaten raw or gently cooked. Chayote has a wrinkled green skin and a creamy white flesh on the inside. When chayote is combined with peppery radishes and watercress and tossed with a mango vinaigrette, the results are an elegant first-course salad.

MAKES 4 SERVINGS

vinaigrette:

1 mango, peeled, pitted, and sliced

½ cup white wine vinegar

¼ cup extra-virgin olive oil

½ teaspoon sugar

¼ teaspoon salt

freshly ground black pepper

salad:

2 bunches of watercress, stems removed

1 chayote, peeled and cut into 1-inch cubes

3 medium radishes, thinly sliced

1. To prepare the vinaigrette, puree the mango, vinegar, oil, sugar, and salt in a blender until smooth. Season with the pepper. Pour the vinaigrette into a small bowl, cover, and refrigerate until ready to serve.

2. To prepare the salad, combine the watercress, chayote, and radishes. Add half of the vinaigrette and toss well. Serve the salad with the remaining dressing passed on the side.

mango, avocado, and spinach salad with poppy seed dressing

Mangoes and avocados: the two fruits I simply can't live without. And I'm always creating new ways to combine sweet mango and buttery avocado in my kitchen. Here, my two faves—along with spinach and pistachios—are tossed with a perky poppy seed, lime juice, and honey dressing. Serve this salad as a first course with grilled seafood or chicken.

MAKES 6 SERVINGS

dressing:

¼ cup extra-virgin olive oil

2 tablespoons lime juice

2 teaspoons honey

1 tablespoon poppy seeds

1 teaspoon cider vinegar

1 teaspoon Dijon mustard

¼ teaspoon cayenne pepper

kosher salt

freshly ground black pepper

salad:

2 large mangoes, peeled, pitted, and cut into ½-inch cubes

2 ripe Hass avocados, halved, pitted, peeled, and cut into ½-inch cubes

½ cup fresh cilantro, coarsely chopped

1 cup shelled pistachios, lightly toasted and chopped

1 5-ounce bag baby spinach

freshly grated zest of 1 lime

1. To make the dressing, combine the olive oil, lime juice, honey, poppy seeds, cider vinegar, mustard, and cayenne pepper in a medium jar with a tight-fitting lid. Shake well until thickened. Season with salt and pepper.

2. To make the salad, combine the mangoes, avocados, cilantro, and half of the pistachios in a medium bowl. Add the dressing and toss well to coat.

3. Put the spinach in a large serving bowl and top with mango-avocado mixture. Toss gently until combined. Sprinkle with the lime zest and the remaining pistachios. Serve immediately.

frisée salad with figs, hazelnuts, and manchego with guava vinaigrette

Frisée, also known as curly endive, has a slightly peppery and spicy essence that adds color, flavor, texture, and nutrition to mixed salads. For a tropical, tangy twist, I toss frisée with a double dose of guava—nectar and paste—vinaigrette and then top the green with fresh figs, toasted hazelnuts, and some Manchego cheese.

MAKES 6 SERVINGS

vinaigrette:

¼ cup guava nectar

2 tablespoons sherry wine vinegar

2 tablespoons extra-virgin olive oil

1 1-inch-long × ¼-inch-thick piece guava paste, cut into cubes

1 shallot, quartered

1 teaspoon honey

kosher salt

freshly ground black pepper

salad:

1 head frisée (curly endive), chopped (about 10 cups)

⅓ cup lightly toasted and skinned hazelnuts, coarsely chopped

6 fresh Mission figs, stems removed, quartered

3 ounces aged Manchego, shaved with a vegetable peeler

1. To make the vinaigrette, puree the guava nectar, vinegar, olive oil, guava paste, shallot, and honey in a blender. Blend until the dressing is smooth and creamy. Season with salt and pepper.

2. To make the salad, put the frisée in a large salad bowl. Add half of the vinaigrette and toss gently to coat. Distribute the hazelnuts, figs, and Manchego evenly on top of the dressed frisée. Toss again and serve immediately, with the remaining dressing on the side.

CHICA TIP

Sweet guava is high in pectin, a naturally occurring jelling and thickening agent also found in apples and quince. As a result, guavas are often cooked with sugar and water into a thick paste that is firm enough to slice. If you can't find guava paste, substitute guava jam or marmalade.

classic latin avocado and tomato salad

This delectable salad proves that seasonal ingredients taste best with little fuss. Avocados and tomatoes take center stage when drizzled with this vibrant vinaigrette and seasoned simply with kosher salt, freshly cracked black pepper, and a flurry of cilantro leaves. I change up this salad throughout the summer season, using a colorful variety of heirloom tomatoes, tossing in some black beans or corn kernels, or replacing the scallions with thinly sliced red onions. It also makes a great sandwich filling for the vegetarians in your life.

MAKES 6 SERVINGS

2 Hass avocados, peeled, pitted, and cut into 1-inch chunks

2 medium tomatoes, cored and cut in 1-inch chunks

4 scallions, white and green parts, cut into ½-inch lengths

1 cup fresh cilantro, coarsely chopped

3 hard-boiled eggs, peeled and cut into ½-inch dice

1 jalapeño, seeded, ribbed, and finely chopped

3 tablespoons distilled white vinegar

kosher salt

freshly ground black pepper

1 head of Boston or Bibb lettuce, leaves separated into cups

1. Gently mix the avocados, tomatoes, scallions, cilantro, eggs, and jalapeño in a medium bowl. Drizzle the vinegar over the mixture and toss gently, seasoning with salt and pepper.

2. To serve, place a lettuce cup on each plate and fill each with equal amounts of the salad. Serve immediately.

shrimp and mango adobado salad with roasted corn avocado salsa

I'm a bit of a rebel in the kitchen, and I like to dream up new ways to reinvent classic dishes. Remember when salsa was made only with tomatoes? Now varieties include everything from pineapple and peppers to corn and carrots. So I came up with this lively corn–red onion–avocado-pepper salsa to go with grilled shrimp and mango skewers. The skewers are briefly immersed in a snappy grapefruit-lime juice marinade.

MAKES 4 SERVINGS

wooden skewers

marinade:

4 garlic cloves

1 teaspoon kosher salt

2 teaspoons ground cumin

2 teaspoons sweet paprika

1 teaspoon dried oregano

pinch of cayenne pepper

1 cup fresh grapefruit juice

¼ cup fresh lime juice

2 tablespoons extra-virgin olive oil

freshly ground black pepper

2 pounds jumbo shrimp, peeled and deveined, tails left intact

2 large firm mangoes, fruit cut from seeds, peeled, and sliced into long wedges

salsa:

4 ears corn, husks and corn silk discarded

3 tablespoons extra-virgin olive oil

kosher salt

freshly ground black pepper

2 ripe Hass avocados, seeded, peeled, and cubed

1 small red onion, finely chopped

1 red bell pepper, cored, seeded, and finely chopped

1 jalapeño pepper, seeded and finely minced

3 tablespoons fresh cilantro or basil leaves, chopped, plus more for garnish

2 tablespoons fresh lime juice

2 tablespoons red wine vinegar

6 cups mixed salad greens or baby spinach

going green: salads

1. Put wooden skewers in a pan of water for 30 minutes so they don't burn on the grill.

2. To make the marinade, coarsely chop the garlic on a cutting board. Sprinkle with the salt and mash the garlic into a paste with the side of the knife. Transfer the garlic paste to a medium bowl. Add the cumin, paprika, oregano, and cayenne and mix. Stir in the grapefruit juice, lime juice, and oil. Season with the pepper.

3. Drain the soaked skewers. Thread the shrimp onto skewers, and repeat with the mango on separate skewers. Put in a glass or ceramic 9 × 13 inch baking dish. Pour about a third of the marinade over the skewers. Cover and refrigerate the remaining marinade to dress the salad. Cover the baking dish with plastic wrap and refrigerate, flipping the skewers occasionally, for no more than 30 minutes.

4. To prepare the salsa, rub the corn with 2 tablespoons of the oil and season with salt and pepper. Preheat an outdoor grill or grill pan to medium high (or preheat a broiler). Put the corn directly on the grill grates (or on the rack of a broiler pan) and cook until the kernels are slightly charred on all sides, turning every couple of minutes. Remove from the heat. Using a sharp knife, stand each cob on its wide end and carefully cut the kernels off of the cobs. Transfer the kernels to a large bowl. Add the avocado, onion, red pepper, jalapeño, cilantro, lime juice, and vinegar. Season with salt and pepper.

5. Grill (or broil) the shrimp, turning once, until opaque and slightly charred on both sides, about 2 to 3 minutes. Cook the mangoes until grill marks appear, about 1 minute on each side.

6. Divide the greens evenly among 4 dinner plates. Drizzle the reserved marinade over the greens. Top each with equal amounts of the shrimp and mango skewers and a couple of spoonfuls of the roasted corn and avocado salsa. Sprinkle with the cilantro and serve with remaining salsa on the side.

CHICA TIP

If using bamboo skewers, soak them in water in a shallow dish for 30 minutes before threading food onto them.

farmers' market roasted vegetable salad in avocado cups

When lightly tossed with a bit of olive oil and then oven roasted, vegetables become oh so sweet, crisp outside, tender inside, and caramelized. Once you try this method, I promise you won't even think about cooking vegetables any other way. Best of all, the vegetables can be served hot or at room temperature. For a colorful Latin touch and an irresistible presentation, I pile the vegetables into avocado halves.

MAKES 6 SERVINGS

4 medium carrots, cut into ½-inch rounds and half-rounds

1 medium zucchini, cut into ½-inch rounds

1 medium yellow squash, cut into ½-inch rounds

1 medium red bell pepper, cored, seeded, ribbed, and cut into ½-inch pieces

3 tablespoons olive oil

kosher salt

1 ear corn, husks removed

3 tablespoons fresh lemon juice

2 tablespoons fresh parsley, chopped

2 tablespoons fresh dill, finely chopped

2 tablespoons fresh chives, finely chopped

freshly ground black pepper

3 Hass avocados

3 to 4 cups arugula or mixed greens (optional)

freshly grated zest of 1 lemon

1. Preheat the oven to 350°F.

2. Mix the carrots, zucchini, squash, and bell pepper in a large bowl. Add 2 tablespoons of oil and toss to coat. Season with the salt. Spread evenly on a large rimmed baking sheet. Bake, stirring occasionally, until the vegetables soften, about 15 minutes. Transfer to a large bowl and let cool.

3. Stand the corn ear on its wide end on a plate or in a wide shallow bowl. Using a small knife, slice downward at the juncture of the kernels and cob to remove the kernels. Work your way around the cob, slicing until all the kernels are removed. You should have about 1½ cups of corn kernels.

4. In a large bowl, mix the cooled vegetables, corn, lemon juice, remaining 1 tablespoon olive oil, parsley, dill, and chive. Season with salt and pepper.

5. Wash the avocados well. Divide the arugula, if using, among six plates. Top each with an avocado half and spoon a generous amount of the vegetables into the avocado. Sprinkle with lemon zest and serve immediately.

grilled romaine salad

Grilling romaine hearts imparts a light flavor to this classic salad. The key is to grill the romaine halves until just charred on the outsides. Top the just-wilted leaves with an oregano-garlic dressing and shavings of salty Parmesan.

MAKES 6 SERVINGS

dressing:

2 garlic cloves

salt

2 tablespoons red wine vinegar

2 tablespoons water

1 tablespoon fresh oregano leaves, finely chopped

½ teaspoon sugar

¼ cup extra-virgin olive oil

freshly ground black pepper

3 heads romaine lettuce, cut lengthwise in half

½ cup Parmesan curls, shaved from a block of cheese with a swivel vegetable peeler

1. Build a medium-hot fire in an outdoor grill or heat a grill pan over high heat.

2. To make the dressing, finely chop the garlic on a chopping board. Sprinkle with a large pinch of salt, and smear the garlic on the chopping board to make a paste. Transfer to a small bowl. Add the vinegar, water, oregano, and sugar and whisk to combine. Gradually whisk in the oil. Season with salt and pepper.

3. If using an outdoor grill, brush the cooking grate clean. Brush the romaine lettuce with some dressing on both sides. Place on the grill or grill pan, cut side down, and grill, turning once, until the lettuce is seared with grill marks, about 2 minutes.

4. Place each romaine half on a dinner plate. Sprinkle with the Parmesan and serve immediately.

fresh herbs and lettuce salad

Another way I avoid BSS (Boring Salad Syndrome) is to add lots of fresh chopped herbs and a sprinkle of crumbled *queso fresco* to lettuces. Here, I use fresh oregano and dill but consider others, such as parsley, basil, chives, mint, and chervil. Although this salad is simple to put together, it's complex in flavor and texture.

MAKES 4 SERVINGS

2 tablespoons fresh lemon juice

¼ cup olive oil

kosher salt

freshly ground black pepper

2 romaine lettuce heads, cut crosswise into thin strips

½ cup *queso fresco* or reduced-fat feta, crumbled

¼ cup fresh dill leaves, coarsely chopped

¼ cup fresh oregano leaves, coarsely chopped

1. Put the lemon juice in a small bowl. Gradually whisk in the oil. Season with salt and pepper and whisk again.

2. Combine the lettuce, *queso fresco*, dill, and oregano in a large bowl. Add the lemon dressing and toss well. Serve immediately.

artichokes, asparagus, and watercress salad with cumin vinaigrette

With a little help from some canned artichoke hearts from your pantry, you can create this gorgeous shades-of-green salad. A no-fuss dressing of apple cider vinegar, Dijon mustard, cumin, and olive oil gives a tangy pop to this gorgeous salad.

MAKES 4 TO 6 SERVINGS

vinaigrette:

2 tablespoons apple cider vinegar

1 teaspoon ground cumin

1 teaspoon sugar

½ teaspoon Dijon mustard

¼ cup extra-virgin olive oil

kosher salt

freshly ground black pepper

salad:

1 bunch asparagus, woody ends snapped off

1 cup fresh flat-leaf parsley, coarsely chopped

1 12-ounce can artichoke hearts, drained and cut into halves lengthwise

1 bunch watercress, tough stems removed

1 medium tomato, cored and chopped

1. To make the vinaigrette, whisk the vinegar, cumin, sugar, and mustard in a small bowl. Gradually whisk in the oil. Season with salt and pepper.

2. To prepare the salad, bring a large saucepan of salted water to a boil over medium-high heat. Fill a large bowl with ice water. Add the asparagus to the boiling water and cook until just tender, about 3 minutes. Drain the asparagus in a colander and then immediately transfer to the ice water. Let stand 1 minute. Drain again and place on a paper towel–lined plate to dry. Cut each asparagus stalk into thirds.

3. Combine the asparagus, parsley, artichokes, watercress, and tomato. Whisk the vinaigrette to recombine. Pour over the salad and toss gently. Serve immediately.

CHICA TIP

I avoid boring salad syndrome by keeping my pantry stocked with canned artichoke hearts, jars of roasted red and yellow peppers, and packages of sun-dried tomatoes. Many supermarkets now have olive bars, so buy a variety of olives. Toss them with some lemon zest, a sprinkling of oregano or thyme, and some fruity olive oil. They'll keep in the refrigerator for months. No boring salads at your table!

going green: salads

campfire *(fogata)* salad

I call this campfire—*fogata* in Spanish—salad because the blanched asparagus spears lean against each other in a triangle like logs on an outdoor fire. The orange carrots, green asparagus, and black beans create a beautiful palette and plate. Serve as a first course, followed by Mirin and Garlic Pan-steamed Salmon (page 203) or Whole Fish Baked in Salt (page 215).

MAKES 4 SERVINGS

vinaigrette:

¼ cup sherry wine vinegar

2 tablespoons extra-virgin olive oil

2 tablespoons minced fresh oregano

1 teaspoon sugar

kosher salt

freshly ground black pepper

salad:

16 to 20 asparagus spears, ends trimmed

1 pound fresh green beans, cut into 1-inch pieces

3 large carrots, shredded (about 2 cups)

1 cup canned black beans, drained and rinsed

1. To make the vinaigrette, whisk together the vinegar, oil, oregano, and sugar. Season with salt and pepper.

2. To make the salad, bring a large pot of water to a boil. Fill a large bowl with ice water. Add the asparagus to the boiling water and cook until tender, about 3 to 5 minutes, depending on their size. Using tongs, remove the asparagus from the water and transfer to the ice water to stop them from cooking. Drain and then transfer to a paper towel–lined baking sheet to dry.

3. Add the green beans to the boiling water and cook just until tender, about 4 to 7 minutes. Fill the large bowl with fresh ice water. Drain the beans in a colander; then immediately put them in the ice water to stop them from cooking. Drain again and pat dry with paper towels.

4. Combine the carrots, black beans, and green beans in a mixing bowl. Drizzle with half the vinaigrette and mix thoroughly.

5. For each salad, spoon a fourth of the carrot mixture in a mound in the middle of the plate. Build a "campfire" by leaning 4 to 5 asparagus spears around the salad. Drizzle with the remaining vinaigrette and serve immediately.

Indulge!

eggplant and fennel salad with warm bacon vinaigrette

Although I don't eat bacon very often, I do find myself missing its smoky, slightly sweet, and—okay, I'll say it—fatty flavor every once in a while. To indulge, I add a bit of bacon to this roasted eggplant and fennel salad for a guilty pleasure. Enjoy this for a weekend main course lunch or as a first course followed by Surf and Turf Romesco (page 131) or Chicken Chorizo Cazuela (page 140).

MAKES 6 SERVINGS

cooking spray

1 eggplant (about 1 pound), cut into ½-inch-thick strips

1 fennel bulb, fronds discarded, cored and thinly sliced

¼ cup olive oil plus 2 tablespoons for roasting

1 garlic clove, minced

½ plus ¼ teaspoon salt

6 slices center-cut bacon, diced

1 shallot, minced

¼ cup red wine vinegar

1 head frisée (curly endive), torn into bite-size pieces (about 6 cups)

½ cup pine nuts, toasted (page 10)

2 tablespoons fresh mint leaves, chopped

1. Spray a large baking pan with cooking spray. Put a broiler rack about 6 inches from the source of heat and preheat the broiler.

2. Combine the eggplant, fennel, 2 tablespoons of oil, garlic, and ½ teaspoon salt in a large bowl; toss to coat. Spread the eggplant-fennel mixture in a single layer in the pan. Broil until the vegetables are tender, stirring halfway through cooking (about 8 minutes). Transfer the pan to a wire rack and let the vegetables cool.

3. Meanwhile, in a medium nonstick skillet over medium-high heat cook the bacon, stirring occasionally, until crisp, about 6 minutes. Using tongs, transfer the bacon to paper towels to drain. Pour off all but 3 tablespoons of drippings in the skillet and return to medium heat. Add the shallot and cook, stirring occasionally, until tender, about 2 minutes. Remove the pan from the heat. Stir in the vinegar, the remaining ¼ cup oil, and the remaining ¼ teaspoon salt and bring to a boil. Remove from the heat and let cool slightly.

4. Combine the frisée, pine nuts, and mint in a large bowl. Drizzle with half of the warm dressing and toss to coat well. Arrange the frisée mixture on a platter. Top with the eggplant mixture. Sprinkle with the bacon and drizzle with the remaining dressing. Serve warm.

smoked paprika roasted chicken

chicken and turkey every which way

Chicken is so versatile and such a great source of protein, it's no wonder that Americans consume more chicken annually than any other meat. But because it's so popular, chicken producers have, over the years, given the birds feed laced with hormones and antibiotics to grow them bigger and more quickly, which isn't good for us. I recommend buying and cooking organic chicken. It tastes better, and it is better for you. Yes, organic chickens might cost more, but eating cleaner food will keep us healthy and save us money by reducing our future medical expenses. I buy organic birds whenever possible.

I prepare chicken so often that I'm always looking for ways to switch it up and give it different Latin twists. This chapter is filled with great healthy chicken recipes inspired by the flavors of Latin America and Spain. I've also included a few turkey recipes at the end of the chapter to keep dinner interesting.

delia's pulled chicken

Delia Leon is my dear friend as well as the producer and vice president of my company. Delia's mom (also named Delia), who lives in Ocala, Florida, often makes batches of this comforting pulled chicken dish and freezes it in plastic bags. She packs the bags in a cooler and asks anyone driving to Miami to deliver it to us. When I asked her for the recipe, I was surprised by how quick and easy it is to make. I was sure it took hours for the chicken to become tender and easily shredded. Serve the chicken with a baked sweet potato or some steamed brown rice.

MAKES 4 TO 6 SERVINGS

1 pound boneless, skinless chicken breast halves, trimmed of excess fat, rinsed

3 cups water

¾ teaspoon Delicioso Adobo Seasoning (page 8)

kosher salt

1 tablespoon olive oil

1 small yellow onion, chopped

2 garlic cloves, minced

4 scallions, green and white parts, chopped

1 medium tomato, cored, seeded, and diced

¼ cup fresh cilantro, chopped, plus more for serving

½ teaspoon dried oregano

¼ teaspoon ground cumin

⅛ teaspoon sugar

freshly ground black pepper

1. Bring the chicken, water, adobo, and ½ teaspoon salt to a boil in a medium saucepan over high heat. Simmer until the chicken is opaque when pierced in the thickest part with the tip of a knife, about 15 minutes. Transfer the chicken to a cutting board. Strain the cooking liquid into a heatproof bowl and reserve. Let the chicken cool. Using two forks, shred the chicken into bite-size pieces.

2. Heat the oil in a large skillet over medium-high heat. Add the onion and garlic and cook, stirring often, until softened and fragrant but not brown, about 2 minutes. Lower heat to medium and add the scallions, tomato, cilantro, oregano, cumin, and sugar. Stir in ¾ cup of the reserved cooking liquid. Bring to a simmer, reduce the heat to medium low, and simmer until the liquid has reduced slightly, about 10 minutes. Add the shredded chicken with another ¾ cup of broth, and season with salt and pepper. Simmer until heated through, about 5 more minutes. Sprinkle with the cilantro and serve hot.

enchiladas *suizas*

Swiss-style enchiladas show how culinary influences can travel great distances and become part of another country's cuisine. It is believed that when people from Switzerland immigrated to Mexico, they established dairy farms and introduced milk- and cream-based sauces to the local food. Such a dish is described as *suizas*, the most popular being enchiladas *suizas*. Too often enchiladas *suizas* are heavy with too much cheese. My lighter version uses chicken, a tomatillo sauce, and reduced-fat cheeses. Same bold flavors with fewer calories and fat.

MAKES 4 TO 6 SERVINGS

1 pound boneless, skinless chicken breast halves, trimmed of excess fat, rinsed

3 cups water

3 garlic cloves, crushed under a knife and peeled

1 teaspoon Delicioso Adobo Seasoning (page 8)

6 medium tomatillos (about 12 ounces), husked, rinsed, and quartered

½ medium yellow onion, coarsely chopped

¼ cup packed cilantro leaves, plus more for garnish

2 jalapeños, seeded and coarsely chopped

½ cup fat-free sour cream

2 tablespoons freshly grated Parmesan cheese

8 corn tortillas

cooking spray

1 cup (4 ounces) 2% milk reduced-fat mozzarella cheese, shredded

1. Place the chicken, water, 2 of the garlic cloves, and the adobo to a boil in a medium saucepan over high heat. Reduce the heat to low and cover. Simmer until the chicken is opaque when pierced in the thickest part with the tip of a knife, about 15 minutes. Transfer the chicken to a cutting board. Strain the cooking liquid into a heatproof bowl and reserve. Let the chicken cool. Using two forks, shred the chicken into bite-size pieces.

2. Puree the tomatillos, onion, cilantro, jalapeños, and the remaining garlic clove with ¼ cup of the reserved cooking liquid. Transfer to a medium saucepan. Bring to a boil over high heat. Reduce the heat to low and simmer, stirring often, until slightly thickened, about 10 minutes. Remove from the heat. Stir in the sour cream and Parmesan. Pour into a wide, shallow dish or bowl.

3. Wrap the tortillas in moistened paper towels. Microwave on high (100%) until the tortillas are pliable, about 15 seconds.

4. Position the broiler rack 6 inches from the source of heat and preheat the broiler. Spray a 9 × 13-inch flameproof baking dish with cooking spray. Dip each tortilla in the sauce. Transfer to a plate. Place about 2 tablespoons of the chicken on the tortilla and roll it up. Place, seam side down, in the baking dish. Pour the remaining sauce over the enchiladas and sprinkle with the mozzarella cheese.

5. Broil until the cheese is melted, about 1 minute. Sprinkle with the cilantro and serve immediately.

CHICA TIP

! Be sure to warm the tortillas before filling and rolling them so they don't break.

chicken and turkey every which way

fajita chicken salad with jalapeño-citrus vinaigrette

So simple but so good—a refreshing salad with pieces of chicken, vegetables, and a citrus vinaigrette with a Latin touch. When the thermometer climbs in the summer, make this with leftover chicken.

MAKES 4 SERVINGS

vinaigrette:

¼ cup fresh orange juice

1 tablespoon fresh lime juice

2 teaspoons fresh mint leaves, chopped

1 teaspoon olive oil

1 teaspoon honey

½ jalapeño, seeded and minced

¼ teaspoon kosher salt

salad:

4 boneless, skinless chicken breast halves, trimmed of excess fat, rinsed, and patted dry

1 teaspoon olive oil

1 teaspoon Delicioso Adobo Seasoning (page 8)

6 cups mixed baby greens

1 medium red bell pepper, cored, seeded, ribbed, and thinly sliced

1 medium yellow bell pepper, cored, seeded, ribbed, and thinly sliced

1 tomato, cored, seeded, and diced

1 ripe Hass avocado, pitted, peeled, and diced

1. To make the vinaigrette, whisk the orange juice, lime juice, mint, 1 teaspoon oil, honey, jalapeño, and salt together in a small bowl.

2. Season the chicken on both sides with the seasoning. Heat the remaining 1 teaspoon oil in a large nonstick skillet over medium-high heat. Add the chicken and cook, turning halfway through cooking, until lightly browned and barely opaque when pierced with the tip of a knife in the thickest part, about 12 minutes. Transfer the chicken to a cutting board. Let stand 5 minutes. Cut crosswise into ½-inch-thick strips.

3. Combine the mixed greens and bell peppers in a large serving bowl. Top with the chicken strips, tomato, and avocado. Drizzle with the vinaigrette, toss gently, and serve immediately.

pipián chicken in acorn squash bowls

Pipián is a mole-like sauce from Mexico that is poured over shredded chicken or enchiladas. Toasted and pureed pumpkin seeds give *pipián* its bright green color. I love to see the looks of delight on my guests' faces when I serve this in cooked acorn squash halves.

MAKES 6 SERVINGS

squash:

cooking spray

3 acorn squash, halved, seeded, and ¼ inch trimmed from skin side to keep squash from rolling

chicken:

12 boneless, skinless chicken thighs, trimmed of excess fat

1 quart water

1 large yellow onion, halved

½ cup packed fresh cilantro, plus more for serving

6 garlic cloves, crushed and peeled

2 teaspoons kosher salt

¼ teaspoon ground cumin

2 bay leaves

2 cups pumpkin seeds (*pepitas*)

6 black peppercorns

¼ cup olive oil

1½ cups store-bought mild green salsa

1. To prepare the squash, preheat the oven to 400°F. Spray a large baking pan with nonstick spray. Put the squash, cut side down, on the pan. Bake, turning once halfway through cooking time, until tender when pierced with the tip of a sharp knife, about 40 minutes. Remove from the oven and tent with aluminum foil to keep warm.

2. Meanwhile, to make the chicken, bring the chicken, water, onion, cilantro, garlic, salt, cumin, and bay leaves to a boil in a large saucepan over high heat. Reduce the heat to medium low and simmer, uncovered, turning the chicken occa-

chicken and turkey every which way

sionally, until the meat is opaque when pierced with the tip of a knife, 15 to 20 minutes. Transfer the chicken to a cutting board and let cool. Reserve 1½ cups of the cooking liquid. Discard the remaining cooking liquid and the solids. When the chicken is cool enough to handle, finely shred, using two forks to pull the meat apart. Transfer to a large bowl and set aside.

3. Spread the pumpkin seeds and peppercorns in a single layer in a large heavy skillet. Cook over medium heat, shaking the skillet frequently, until the seeds are toasted, fragrant, and slightly puffed, about 3 minutes. Transfer to a plate and set aside to cool. When cool, transfer the pumpkin seeds and peppercorns to a food processor and pulse until ground. Reserve 2 tablespoons of the mixture for garnish later.

4. Heat the oil in a large nonstick skillet over medium-high heat. Add the pumpkin seed mixture to the skillet and cook, stirring frequently, until the mixture just begins to brown, about 5 minutes. Slowly stir in the reserved cooking liquid and the salsa, and bring to a boil. Reduce the heat to medium low and simmer, uncovered, stirring occasionally, until the sauce begins to thicken, about 5 minutes. Stir in the shredded chicken and cook until heated through, about 2 minutes. For each serving, place a squash half on a dinner plate. Spoon the chicken mixture into each squash half, and sprinkle with the cilantro and reserved pumpkin seed mixture. Serve hot.

CHICA TIP

Any small winter squash—delicate, pumpkin, or buttercup—can be used in place of acorn squash.

adobo-grilled chicken salad in tortilla bowls

Instead of deep-frying tortillas to make bowls, I drape whole-wheat flour tortillas over recycled cans and bake them into sturdy tortilla bowls. The edible vessels are filled with leafy greens and smothered with warm pinto beans coated in thick chipotle-tomato sauce. Grilled and sliced chicken with adobo seasoning is fanned on top, followed by a sprinkle of feta. Start saving those empty 15-ounce cans!

MAKES 4 SERVINGS

4 boneless, skinless chicken breasts, trimmed of excess fat, rinsed, and patted dry

1 tablespoon Delicioso Adobo Seasoning (page 8)

canola oil cooking spray

salad:

4 10-inch whole-wheat or multigrain tortillas

2 tablespoons olive oil, plus more for drizzling

½ medium yellow onion, chopped

4 garlic cloves, minced

kosher salt

freshly ground black pepper

3 medium tomatoes, cored, seeded, and chopped

½ cup water

2 chipotle chiles in adobo, chopped, plus 2 tablespoons of the adobo sauce

1 15-ounce can pinto beans, drained and rinsed

5 cups baby spinach leaves or mixed mesclun greens

½ cup (2 ounces) reduced-fat feta, crumbled

¼ cup fresh cilantro, chopped

lime wedges, for serving

1. Season chicken breasts with the adobo seasoning. Spray a ridged grill pan with the cooking spray and heat over medium heat. Add the chicken and cook, turning halfway through cooking, until lightly browned and barely opaque when pierced with the tip of a knife in the thickest part, about 12 minutes. Transfer the chicken to a cutting board. Let stand until cooled. Cut crosswise into ½-inch-thick strips.

2. To prepare the bowls, preheat the oven to 400°F. Place a small dish of water next to your work surface. To make the tortilla bowls, place four empty 15-ounce cans, open side down, on a baking pan. Using a pastry brush, soften the tortillas by brushing both sides with a little water, and then brush them with 1 tablespoon of oil. Drape the tortillas over the cans and bake until firm, about 5 to 7 minutes. Using tongs, turn the tortilla bowls right side up, discard the cans, and continue to bake until golden and crisp, another 4 minutes.

3. Heat the remaining tablespoon of oil in a large skillet over medium heat. Add the onion

chicken and turkey every which way

and cook, stirring occasionally until tender and translucent, about 4 minutes. Stir in the garlic and cook until fragrant, about 1 minute. Season with salt and pepper. Add the tomatoes, water, and chipotles with adobo sauce. Bring to a boil and cook, stirring occasionally, until thickened, about 5 minutes. Stir in the beans and cook until heated through, about 3 minutes. Remove from the heat.

4. Place the tortilla bowls right side up on plates and fill each with a handful of greens. Divide the bean mixture among the tortilla bowls and top with a sprinkle of feta. Fan the sliced chicken on top and garnish with chopped cilantro. Drizzle with a little olive oil and serve with lime wedges.

quick chicken mole poblano

Making traditional, authentic mole is time consuming and labor intensive; lots of spices and chiles are roasted, ground by hand, and then slowly cooked with water into a thick paste. My quick-and-easy Puebla-style mole is made with fewer ingredients and pureed in a blender. Once the sauce is done, I shred a store-bought rotisserie chicken and add it to the sauce. Mole keeps indefinitely in the refrigerator so you can pick up a cooked chicken on the way home and have dinner ready in no time.

MAKES 4 TO 6 SERVINGS

2 tablespoons olive oil

1 medium yellow onion, chopped

3 garlic cloves, minced

1 15-ounce can diced tomatoes with juices

1 cup dark raisins

1 chipotle pepper with 1 teaspoon adobo sauce (or more to taste), chopped

2 cups low-sodium chicken broth

3 tablespoons smooth peanut butter

2 teaspoons chili powder

½ teaspoon ground cinnamon

kosher salt

freshly ground black pepper

1½ ounces unsweetened chocolate, coarsely chopped, or 2 tablespoons unsweetened cocoa powder

1 store-bought rotisserie chicken, meat removed and shredded, skin and bones discarded

¼ cup peanuts, coarsely chopped, for garnish

1 teaspoon sesame seeds, for garnish

zest of 1 orange, for garnish

1 ripe Hass avocado, peeled, pitted, and sliced, for serving

fresh cilantro, for serving

lime wedges, for serving

4 8-inch whole-wheat or multigrain tortillas, warmed, for serving

1. Heat the oil in a large saucepan over medium heat. Add the onion and garlic and cook, stirring occasionally, until softened, about 5 minutes. Add the tomatoes, raisins, and chipotle with adobo and stir to combine. Bring to a simmer, reduce the heat to medium-low, and cook for 10 minutes.

2. Carefully pour the mixture into a blender. Add the broth, peanut butter, chili powder, and cinnamon. Puree the mixture until smooth. Season with salt and pepper.

3. Return the mixture to the saucepan and bring to a simmer over medium heat. Cook, stirring occasionally, until slightly thickened, about 15 minutes. Add the chocolate and stir until melted. (The mole sauce can be made up to this point and refrigerated. Reheat before using.) Add the shredded chicken and heat through.

4. Transfer the mole to a serving dish and sprinkle with the peanuts, sesame seeds, and orange zest. Serve with bowls of the avocado, cilantro, lime wedges, and tortillas for guests to add to their serving.

pineapple-chicken skewers with passion fruit glaze

Fire up the grill for marinated chicken chunks, red onions, bell peppers, and pineapple cubes threaded onto skewers, thickly painted with a sweet-and-sour passion fruit glaze. Grilled Romaine Salad (page 107) is the perfect accompaniment.

MAKES 6 SERVINGS

chicken:

½ cup olive oil

4 3-inch sprigs rosemary

5 3-inch sprigs oregano

4 garlic cloves, crushed and peeled

kosher salt

freshly ground black pepper

2 pounds boneless, skinless chicken breasts cut into 24 2-inch pieces

passion fruit glaze:

½ cup passion fruit nectar

2 tablespoons ketchup

1 tablespoon fresh lime juice

1 tablespoon soy sauce

1½ teaspoons honey

kosher salt

freshly ground black pepper

skewers:

1 large red bell pepper, cored, seeded, ribbed, and cut into 24 1-inch pieces

1 medium red onion, cut into 24 1-inch pieces

About ⅔ peeled and cored pineapple, cut into 24 1-inch pieces (save the remaining pineapple for another use)

1 head butter lettuce, leaves separated into cups

1. To prepare the chicken, combine the olive oil, rosemary, oregano, and garlic in a large bowl and season with salt and pepper. Add the chicken and turn to coat. Cover and refrigerate, occasionally turning the chicken, for at least 4 hours or overnight.

2. To prepare the glaze, process the passion fruit nectar, ketchup, lime juice, soy sauce, and honey until smooth. Season with salt and pepper. Blend until well combined. Pour into a small bowl.

3. Preheat a ridged stovetop grill pan over high heat. Remove the chicken from the marinade, discarding the marinade. Alternately thread 3 pieces bell pepper, 3 pieces onion, 3 pieces pineapple, and 4 pieces chicken on each skewer. Place on a platter and repeat process with the remaining ingredients and skewers.

4. Brush the skewers evenly with half of the passion fruit glaze (about 6 tablespoons). Add the skewers to the hot grill pan and cook for 4 to 5 minutes. Turn the skewers and brush them with additional glaze. Cook for another 4 to 5 minutes. (You may have to do this in batches if your grill pan isn't large enough to hold all the skewers at one time.)

5. Serve the skewers on a bed of the lettuce leaves. Brush with additional passion fruit glaze and serve remaining sauce on the side.

surf and turf romesco

Chicken and shrimp come together in this succulent dish inspired from the Catalan region in Spain. Romesco is a nut-based sauce made from toasted almonds, garlic, saffron, parsley, smoked paprika, and olive oil. All of the ingredients are crushed together with a mortar and pestle to give the sauce a rustic texture. To save time, I use a food processor.

MAKES 4 SERVINGS

1 pound boneless, skinless chicken breast halves, trimmed of excess fat, rinsed, and patted dry

1 teaspoon ground cinnamon

1 teaspoon kosher salt

1 teaspoon freshly ground black pepper

3 tablespoons olive oil

16 large shrimp, shelled and deveined (about ¾ pound)

1 medium yellow onion, diced

3 garlic cloves, minced

4 medium tomatoes, cored, seeded, and diced

1 cup dry white wine, such as sauvignon blanc

1 cup low-sodium chicken broth

½ cup sliced almonds, toasted (page 10)

1 slice firm white sandwich bread, toasted and cubed

1 teaspoon smoked paprika

¼ teaspoon saffron threads

1 bay leaf

2 tablespoons fresh flat-leaf parsley, chopped

1. Cut the chicken into 1½-inch chunks. Sprinkle and toss with the cinnamon, ½ teaspoon of salt, and ½ teaspoon of pepper. Heat 2 tablespoons of the oil in a Dutch oven over medium-high heat. Add the chicken and cook, turning occasionally, until browned, 6 to 8 minutes. With a slotted spoon, transfer the chicken to a large bowl.

2. Add the shrimp to the Dutch oven and cook, turning occasionally, over medium-high heat, until the shrimp turn opaque, about 2 minutes. Add the shrimp to the bowl with the chicken.

3. Heat the remaining 1 tablespoon oil in the Dutch oven over medium-high heat. Add the onion and garlic and cook, stirring occasionally, until the onion is tender, about 5 minutes. Add the tomatoes and cook, stirring occasionally, until the tomatoes are soft, about 5 minutes. Add the wine, broth, almonds, bread cubes, paprika, saffron, bay leaf, the remaining ½ teaspoon salt, and ½ teaspoon pepper. Bring to a boil. Reduce the heat and simmer, covered, until the flavors are blended, about 20 minutes.

4. In batches, puree the mixture in a blender with the lid ajar to make a coarse paste. Return to the Dutch oven. Add the chicken and shrimp and cook just until heated through, about 1 minute. Season with salt and pepper. Sprinkle with the parsley.

chicken and turkey every which way

basque-style chicken

My great-grandmother was from Catalonia and my great-grandfather was from the Basque country, both in Northern Spain, so there were frequent culinary influences from both regions in our food at home. Tomatoes, onions, smoked paprika, and serrano ham are the hallmark ingredients of this lively *plat mijoté* (simmered dish) from the Basque region.

MAKES 4 TO 6 SERVINGS

2 pounds thin-sliced chicken breast cutlets

kosher salt

freshly ground black pepper

2 tablespoons olive oil

1 medium white onion, cut into thin half-moons

2 red bell peppers, cored, seeded, ribbed, and cut into ¼-inch-wide strips

4 garlic cloves, minced

1 teaspoon dried thyme

1 14.5-ounce can crushed tomatoes

4 ounces (¼-inch-thick) serrano ham, cut into ¼-inch dice

¼ cup Mediterranean black olives, pitted and sliced

1 teaspoon smoked paprika

¼ teaspoon cayenne pepper

1½ teaspoons dry sherry

½ cup fresh flat-leaf parsley leaves, chopped

1. Season the chicken with salt and pepper. Heat 1 tablespoon olive oil in a large skillet over medium heat. In batches, add the chicken and cook, turning halfway through cooking, until lightly browned but not completely cooked through, about 4 minutes. Transfer to a platter.

2. Add the remaining tablespoon of olive oil. Add the onion, bell pepper, garlic, and thyme to the skillet and cook, stirring occasionally, until softened, about 3 minutes. Add the crushed tomatoes, serano ham, olives, paprika, and cayenne pepper, and stir well, scraping up any browned bits in the skillet, and bring to a simmer. Return the chicken to the skillet. Cook until the chicken is opaque in the center when pierced with the tip of a knife, 2 to 3 minutes.

3. Stir in the sherry. Then add all but 2 tablespoons of the parsley, and cook for 2 minutes to mellow the alcohol flavor. Season the sauce with salt and pepper. Sprinkle with the reserved parsley and serve immediately.

peruvian lemon chicken

When *ají amarillo* is combined with lemon juice and onions, this wonderfully aromatic chicken dish is short on prep and big on flavor.

MAKES 6 SERVINGS

4 boneless, skinless chicken breast halves, trimmed of excess fat, rinsed, and patted dry

salt

freshly ground black pepper

4 tablespoons canola oil

2 pounds medium yellow onions, halved and sliced

1 teaspoon minced garlic

3 tablespoons *ají amarillo* paste (yellow Peruvian chile) or canned mild green chiles

1 cup fresh lemon juice (from 5 to 6 lemons)

1. Season the chicken with salt and pepper. Heat the oil in a large skillet over medium-high heat. Add the chicken and cook, turning halfway through cooking, until golden brown, about 4 minutes. Transfer to a plate.

2. Add the onions and garlic and reduce the heat to medium low. Cook, stirring occasionally, until the onions are golden brown, about 10 minutes. Stir in the *ají amarillo* and season with salt and pepper. Return the chicken to the skillet. Spoon some of the onions over the chicken, cover and cook until the chicken is opaque when pierced in the thickest part with the tip of a knife, 10 to 15 minutes. Add the lemon juice and cook another 5 minutes to allow flavors to meld. Serve immediately.

piña colada chicken tacos

Escape to the tropics with the flavors of piña coladas in these zesty chicken tacos! Rum-and-orange-marinated chicken breasts are sautéed and cut into strips, then topped with pineapple, cucumber, and red onion salsa and wrapped in tortillas. Avocado crema—a puree of avocado and sour cream—and toasted coconut add the final flourish. Be sure to use white balsamic vinegar or seasoned rice vinegar; red will turn the crema pink.

salsa:

1 cup (½-inch dice) fresh pineapple, peeled and cored

1 cup (½-inch dice) cucumber, peeled and seeded

¼ cup red onion, thinly sliced

2 tablespoons fresh flat-leaf parsley, chopped

1 tablespoon white balsamic vinegar

1 tablespoon olive oil

avocado crema:

1 Hass avocado, peeled, pitted, and cut into 1-inch pieces

½ cup fat-free sour cream

1 tablespoon fresh lime juice

¼ teaspoon salt

¼ teaspoon pepper

1 tablespoon fresh ginger, peeled and finely grated

1 tablespoon fresh thyme leaves, chopped

1 tablespoon ground allspice

1 teaspoon honey

½ teaspoon ground cumin

1 garlic clove, minced

½ teaspoon salt

2 teaspoons canola oil

4 boneless, skinless chicken breast halves, trimmed of excess fat, rinsed, and patted dry

2 tablespoons dark rum

8 6-inch whole-wheat tortillas, warmed

1. To make the salsa, toss the ingredients in a glass or ceramic bowl. Cover and let stand for 1 hour to blend the flavors.

2. To make the crema, with a fork, coarsely mash the avocado in a small bowl. Add the sour cream, lime juice, salt, and pepper and stir until well blended. Cover with plastic wrap and refrigerate until ready to serve.

3. Combine the ginger, thyme, allspice, honey, cumin, garlic, and salt in a small bowl until blended. Rub both sides of the chicken with the spice mixture.

4. Heat the oil in a large nonstick skillet over medium-high heat. Add the chicken and cook, turning occasionally, until the chicken is golden brown and is opaque when pierced with the tip of a knife, about 6 minutes. Transfer the chicken to a plate. Reduce the heat to low. Add the rum to the skillet and cook, scraping up the browned bits with a wooden spoon, and bring to a boil. Return the chicken to the skillet, turning to coat both sides in the pan drippings. Transfer to a plate and let cool slightly. When cool enough to handle, using two forks, shred the chicken into bite-size strips.

5. To serve, spoon ¼ of the chicken mixture onto each warm tortilla. Top each with ¼ of the salsa and ¼ of the crema. Fold the opposite sides over to enclose the filling and serve at once.

tequila chicken with chipotle barbecue sauce

Homemade barbecue sauce, without the sugary corn syrup and other unhealthy ingredients found in commercial brands, is a cinch to make. And it keeps well in a jar in the refrigerator for two weeks. My sauce gets its sweetness from prunes. Chipotles in adobo impart some background heat and a smoky flavor. Everyone will be licking their fingers!

MAKES 4 SERVINGS

chicken:

8 boneless, skinless chicken thighs, trimmed of excess fat

1 tablespoon tequila

1 teaspoon kosher salt

1 teaspoon apple cider vinegar

½ teaspoon Delicioso Adobo Seasoning (page 8)

¼ teaspoon freshly ground black pepper

barbecue sauce:

2 teaspoons canola oil

½ medium yellow onion, chopped

2 garlic cloves, chopped

1 cup pitted dried plums (prunes)

1 cup tomato sauce

½ cup packed light brown sugar

1 tablespoon apple cider vinegar

1 tablespoon Dijon mustard

1 tablespoon soy sauce

2 chipotles in adobe, chopped

¼ cup water

½ teaspoon kosher salt

¼ teaspoon freshly ground black pepper

1½ tablespoons canola oil

fresh cilantro, chopped, for garnish

1. To prepare the chicken, combine the chicken, tequila, salt, vinegar, adobo seasoning, and pepper in a large zip-tight plastic bag. Close the bag and refrigerate for 1 hour.

2. Meanwhile, to make the barbecue sauce, heat the canola oil in a medium saucepan over medium heat. Add the onion and cook, stirring occasionally, until the onion is translucent, about 3 minutes. Stir in the garlic. Add the dried plums, tomato sauce, brown sugar, vinegar, mustard, soy sauce, and chipotles and bring to a boil. Reduce the heat to medium low and simmer until the dried plums soften, about 5 minutes. Let cool slightly. Puree in a blender with the lid ajar. Return to the saucepan and stir in the water, salt, and pepper.

3. Preheat the oven to 400°F.

4. Heat the canola oil in a large ovenproof skillet over medium-high heat. Add the chicken and cook, turning halfway through cooking, until golden brown on both sides, about 6 minutes. Pour half of the barbecue sauce over the chicken and cover the skillet with aluminum foil. Bake until the chicken is opaque when pierced in the thickest part with the tip of a knife, 20 to 25 minutes.

5. Transfer to a platter and sprinkle with the chopped cilantro. Serve hot with the remaining sauce passed on the side.

indo-latino noodle bowls

When I was a child, my family and I lived for a time in Holland, where we were introduced to the foods of Indonesia, once a Dutch colony. My mother, who adapted her cooking to wherever we were living, combined Indonesian ingredients like ginger and coconut milk with adobo seasoning for a Latin touch.

MAKES 4 SERVINGS

meatballs:

1 pound ground chicken breast

1 tablespoon finely grated fresh ginger

1 tablespoon Delicioso Adobo Seasoning (page 8)

freshly grated zest of ½ lemon

1 tablespoon peanut oil

2 scallions, white and green parts, thinly cut into diagonal slices (¼ cup plus 2 tablespoons)

3 garlic cloves, thinly sliced

1 jalapeño, cut into thin rounds

1 teaspoon ground cumin

1 cup canned unsweetened coconut milk

½ cup low-sodium chicken broth

½ cup packed fresh cilantro, chopped

1 tablespoon soy sauce

kosher salt

freshly ground black pepper

8 ounces whole-wheat linguine or spaghetti

1. Bring a large pot of lightly salted water to a boil over high heat.

2. To make the meatballs, combine the ground chicken, 1 tablespoon of the ginger, adobo seasoning, and lemon zest in a large bowl until well mixed. Rinse your hands under cold water, and shape the mixture into 28 balls.

3. Heat the oil in a large, deep nonstick skillet over medium-high heat. In batches, add the meatballs, and cook, turning often, until browned, about 8 minutes. Transfer the meatballs to a plate. Return the skillet with the pan juices to medium-high heat.

4. Add ¼ cup of the scallions, the remaining 1 tablespoon ginger, and the garlic, jalapeño, and cumin to the skillet. Cook, stirring constantly, until fragrant, about 1 minute. Stir in the coconut milk, broth, ¼ cup of cilantro, and the soy sauce; bring to a boil. Reduce the heat and simmer, stirring often, until the flavors are blended, about 5 minutes. Return the meatballs to the skillet; bring to a boil. Season with salt and pepper to taste. Reduce the heat and simmer, uncovered, stirring often, until the meatballs are opaque when pierced with the tip of a knife, about 5 minutes. Meanwhile, cook the linguine according to the package instructions.

5. Add the linguine to the skillet, tossing to coat well. Transfer to a platter. Sprinkle with the remaining scallions and cilantro and serve.

chicken and turkey every which way

waldorf chicken lettuce wraps with *nogada* sauce

Nogada, a sauce of chopped walnuts and crema mixed together, is another spectacular dish from the state of Puebla, Mexico, and is traditionally served with chiles. I decided to use *nogada* in place of mayonnaise to give this meal a Latin accent. The result is crisp, clean, sweet, and savory layered with textures and healthy flavors—light but filling.

MAKES 6 SERVINGS

nogada sauce:

1 cup walnut pieces, toasted (page 10)

½ cup reduced-fat sour cream

½ cup 1% low-fat milk

slaw:

1 jicama, peeled, shredded on a V-slicer or the large holes of a box grater, and squeezed dry

4 celery stalks, cut into thin strips with a V-slicer or a knife

2 tablespoons fresh lime juice

¼ teaspoon kosher salt

¼ teaspoon freshly ground black pepper

chicken:

2 pounds chicken tenders, cut into 1-inch pieces

½ teaspoon kosher salt

¼ teaspoon freshly ground black pepper

1 tablespoon olive oil

1 cup seedless red grapes, halved

1 Red Gala apple, peeled, cored, and cut into ½-inch cubes

12 Boston lettuce leaves, rinsed and dried

1. To make the *nogada* sauce, pulse the walnuts, sour cream, and milk together in a food processor until smooth. Transfer to a small bowl. Cover with plastic wrap and refrigerate until ready to serve.

2. To make the slaw, combine the jicama, celery, lime juice, salt, and pepper in a large bowl. Cover with plastic wrap and refrigerate until ready to serve.

3. Season the chicken with the salt and pepper. Heat the oil in a large nonstick skillet over medium-high heat. Add the chicken and cook, stirring occasionally, until browned and opaque when pierced with the tip of a knife, about 5 minutes. Add the grapes and apple and cook, stirring occasionally, until the grapes and apples just begin to soften slightly, about 5 minutes.

4. To serve, divide the chicken mixture evenly among each lettuce leaf. Top each serving with the slaw and a spoonful of sauce. Serve at once, letting each person roll up a lettuce leaf to eat the wrap.

chicken chorizo cazuela

I love this comforting all-in-one rustic stew from Spain. Perfect for a dinner party on a blustery evening accompanied by some crusty bread and rioja wine.

MAKES 6 TO 8 SERVINGS

2 pounds chicken thighs with bone, skin removed

2 pounds chicken drumsticks, skin removed

½ cup all-purpose flour

2 tablespoons olive oil, plus more as needed

8 ounces smoked Spanish chorizo, thinly sliced

1 medium yellow onion, chopped

4 medium carrots, cut into ½-inch rounds

4 celery stalks, cut into ½-inch-wide slices

4 ounces white mushrooms, sliced

3 garlic cloves, minced

1 tablespoon tomato paste

1 28-ounce can chopped tomatoes in juice

1 cup reduced-sodium chicken broth

6 sprigs fresh thyme

3 bay leaves

¼ teaspoon cayenne

1 15-ounce can cannellini (white kidney) beans, drained and rinsed

kosher salt

freshly ground black pepper

1. Sprinkle the chicken thighs and drumsticks evenly with the flour and shake off the excess flour. Heat 2 tablespoons of oil in large Dutch oven over medium-high heat. In batches, add the chicken and cook, turning occasionally, until browned, about 8 minutes. Transfer the chicken to a platter.

2. Add the chorizo, onion, carrots, celery, mushrooms, and garlic. Cook, stirring often, until softened, about 4 minutes. Stir in the tomato paste and mix well to coat the vegetable mixture.

3. Return the chicken to Dutch oven. Stir in the tomatoes and their juices, broth, thyme, bay leaves, and cayenne. Bring to a boil. Cover and reduce the heat to medium low. Simmer for 20 minutes. Uncover and cook, stirring occasionally, until the sauce has thickened and the chicken looks opaque when pierced in the thickest part with the tip of a knife, about 15 minutes more. During the last 5 minutes, stir in the beans. Season with salt and pepper. Serve hot.

smoked paprika roasted chicken

Roast chicken. Shiny, crisp skin. Juicy, tender meat. Sounds so simple, but why is it so difficult to make? I've cooked hundreds of chickens, adjusting the oven's temperature and the cooking times to come up with the perfect bird. First, I rub a paste of smoked paprika, chipotle powder, honey, and a few other ingredients all over and under the skin of the chicken. Then I roast it on a bed of aromatic vegetables until it's done to perfection.

MAKES 4 TO 6 SERVINGS

canola oil cooking spray

1 tablespoon smoked paprika

1 tablespoon chipotle powder

1 tablespoon honey

1 tablespoon fresh lemon juice

2 teaspoons olive oil

2 garlic cloves, minced

½ teaspoon salt

1 4-pound whole chicken

3 celery stalks, cut into 2-inch lengths

3 medium carrots, cut into 2-inch chunks

2 large white onions, quartered

¼ cup reduced-sodium chicken broth

1. Preheat the oven to 400°F. Spray a roasting pan with nonstick spray.

2. Combine the paprika, chipotle powder, honey, lemon juice, oil, garlic, and salt in a small bowl to make a paste.

3. Pat the chicken dry with paper towels. Gently loosen the skin from the breast and leg portions of the chicken by slipping your fingers under the skin. Rub the paste evenly under the skin and on top of the skin. Tuck the wing tips behind the chicken's shoulders and tie the legs together with kitchen string.

4. Make a bed for the chicken with the celery and carrots in the bottom of the pan. Place the chicken, breast side up, on top of the vegetables. Add the onions and broth to the pan. Roast until an Instant Read Thermometer inserted into the thigh (not touching the bone) registers 165°F, about 1 hour 10 minutes. If chicken is browning too fast, cover with aluminum foil.

5. Transfer the chicken to a cutting board and let stand for 10 minutes. Carve the chicken. Remove the chicken skin before eating, if desired. Serve the carved chicken with the roasted vegetables.

chicken and turkey every which way

sherry and parsley chicken
(pollo al jerez)

Jerez, or sherry, is a fortified wine, which means that brandy or another spirit is added to the wine once it has fermented. The best known sherries, ranging from light and dry to dark and sweet, come from Andalucía in southern Spain. They are sipped with tapas or as an after-dinner drink. Dry sherry gives this easy chicken dish a delicate nutty flavor.

3 tablespoons all-purpose flour

½ teaspoon kosher salt

¼ teaspoon freshly ground black pepper

1 pound boneless, skinless chicken breast halves, cut into ¾-inch pieces

3 tablespoons olive oil

3 garlic cloves, minced

⅔ cup dry sherry

⅓ cup reduced-sodium chicken broth

2 tablespoons green olives, pitted and chopped

2 tablespoons nonpareil capers with their brine

1½ teaspoons fresh thyme leaves, finely chopped

1 cup fresh flat-leaf parsley, finely chopped

1 lemon, quartered

1. Combine the flour, salt, and pepper in a large zip-tight plastic bag. Add the chicken and shake to coat the chicken with the flour mixture. Transfer to a plate, shaking off the excess flour.

2. Heat 2 tablespoons of oil in a large nonstick skillet over medium-high heat. Add the chicken and cook, turning halfway through cooking, until golden brown, about 5 minutes. Return to the plate.

3. Reduce the heat to medium. Add the remaining 1 tablespoon of oil and the garlic and cook, stirring often, until fragrant, about 1 minute. (Do not let the garlic burn.) Add the sherry, broth, olives, capers, and thyme and bring to a boil. Return the chicken to the skillet and cook, stirring frequently, over medium heat, until the sauce begins to thicken and the chicken is opaque when pierced in the thickest part with the tip of a knife, 3 to 4 minutes. Remove from the heat and stir in the parsley. Serve hot, with the lemon quarters.

cumin-and-yogurt-roasted turkey breast with tamarind sauce

Boneless turkey breasts are a real time-saver as well as a space saver. Unlike whole turkeys, they need only about an hour to cook and don't take up too much room in the refrigerator. Turkey can be dry, so I massage it under the skin with a spiced yogurt mixture and baste the breast during cooking to keep it moist. Tamarind-ginger-onion is a great alternative to the usual cranberry sauce.

MAKES 6 SERVINGS

turkey:

cooking spray

½ cup nonfat plain Greek yogurt

½ medium white onion, coarsely chopped

2 tablespoons unsalted butter, at room temperature

1 jalapeño, seeded and minced

2 garlic cloves, minced

1 teaspoon ground cumin

kosher salt

pinch of freshly grated nutmeg

1 2-pound boneless turkey breast half with skin

freshly ground black pepper

1 bunch fresh cilantro

¼ cup dark rum

¼ cup water

tamarind sauce:

2 cups water

3 tablespoons tamarind paste

6 tablespoons honey

2 tablespoons olive oil

1 medium yellow onion, finely chopped

3 garlic cloves, minced

½ cup reduced-sodium chicken broth

½ cup fresh cilantro, chopped

2 teaspoons soy sauce

1½ teaspoons ground cumin

1 teaspoon Sriracha sauce

½ teaspoon fresh ginger, peeled and grated

½ teaspoon kosher salt

¼ teaspoon ground cinnamon

1. Preheat the oven to 450°F. Spray a small roasting pan with cooking spray.

2. To prepare the turkey, puree the yogurt, onion, butter, jalapeño, garlic, cumin, ¼ teaspoon salt, and nutmeg together in a food processor.

3. Place the turkey on a work surface, skin side up. Carefully slip your fingers underneath the skin to loosen it from the flesh to create a pocket, keeping the skin attached at one side. Spread half of the yogurt mixture evenly under the skin. Season the turkey generously with salt and pepper.

4. Cut the stems off the cilantro. Chop the leaves, measure ½ cup, and set aside. Spread the cilantro stems in the bottom of the roasting pan. Put the turkey on top of the stems. The heat from the pan will release the oils from the cilantro stems and flavor the breast.

5. Put the roasting pan in the oven and immediately reduce the oven temperature to 400°F. Roast the turkey for 25 minutes. Baste generously

with the remaining yogurt mixture, and continue roasting until an Instant Read Thermometer inserted into the thickest part of breast reads 165°F, about 25 minutes longer. Transfer the turkey to a carving board and cover loosely with aluminum foil to keep warm.

6. Place the roasting pan over two burners on medium heat. Slowly add the rum, scraping up the browned bits in the pan with a wooden spoon. Add ¼ cup of water and boil for 1 minute. Remove from the heat.

7. Meanwhile, to make the gravy, bring the water and tamarind paste to a simmer in a medium saucepan over medium heat, mashing the paste with a fork or potato masher, until the paste softens and begins to dissolve. Reduce the heat to medium-low and simmer for 10 minutes. Strain the tamarind mixture through a small wire sieve into a medium bowl, pressing on the solids with the back of a spoon. Discard the solids in the sieve. Return the strained mixture to the saucepan. Add the honey and simmer until slightly reduced, about 10 minutes. Remove from the heat and set aside.

8. Heat the oil in a large skillet over medium heat. Add the onion and garlic and cook, stirring occasionally, until the onion is softened, about 5 minutes. Add the tamarind mixture, rum pan drippings, broth, ¼ cup of chopped cilantro, soy sauce, cumin, Sriracha, ginger, salt, and cinnamon. Bring to a boil. Reduce the heat to medium-low and simmer briskly, stirring occasionally, until the sauce has reduced to about ½ cup and coats a wooden spoon, about 10 minutes.

9. Carve the turkey across the grain into diagonal slices about ½-inch thick. Transfer to a serving platter. Sprinkle with the remaining cilantro and serve with the sauce.

CHICA TIP

Tamarind is a sweet-and-sour pod from the tree of the same name. You can buy the pods and soak them in water to make pulp, but I use tamarind paste, which is available in brick form or in a small plastic container. Tamarind has a sour-tart flavor and is used to make sauces and drinks. A little bit goes a long way. Look for the paste or frozen tamarind pulp in Asian and Latin markets.

turkey-spinach mini quiches

Wait until you see the smiles at your table when you serve these healthful no-pastry quiches! Individual ramekins are lined with sliced turkey, filled with a quichelike blend of spinach and eggs, and topped with a sprinkle of feta, then baked.

MAKES 4 SERVINGS

4 large eggs plus 4 large egg whites

1 teaspoon fresh oregano leaves, finely chopped

¼ teaspoon sweet paprika

¼ teaspoon kosher salt

¼ teaspoon freshly ground black pepper

1 16-ounce package frozen chopped spinach, thawed, excess water squeezed out

nonstick cooking spray

¾ pound deli-style roasted turkey breast, sliced

¾ cup (3 ounces) reduced-fat feta, crumbled

crushed hot red pepper flakes, for serving (optional)

1. Preheat the oven to 350°F.

2. Whisk the eggs, egg whites, oregano, paprika, salt, and pepper in a large bowl. Stir in the spinach.

3. Lightly coat the insides of 4 6-inch baking dishes with cooking spray. Line each dish with 3 to 4 slices of the sliced turkey, folding the turkey over as needed, to create a sort of bowl or basket inside the dish. Fill each with equal amounts of the egg mixture and sprinkle with the feta.

4. Bake for 25 minutes until a knife inserted in the center of the custard comes out clean, about 25 minutes. Sprinkle with the hot pepper, if desired. Serve warm.

turkey chili

Yes, turkey is lean and low in fat, but that also means that it can be bland. When making turkey chili or any turkey dish, for that matter, I punch up the flavors by adding plenty of onions, garlic, and spices as well as some lager and just a bit of chocolate.

MAKES 4 TO 6 SERVINGS

2 tablespoons olive oil

2 pounds ground turkey breast

2 medium yellow onions, chopped

4 garlic cloves, finely chopped

2 teaspoons chili powder

2 teaspoons ground cumin

1 teaspoon dried oregano

1 14-ounce can chopped tomatoes in juice

1 cup reduced-sodium chicken broth

½ cup lager

1 tablespoon tomato paste

kosher salt

freshly ground black pepper

1 14-ounce can red kidney beans, drained and rinsed

2 ounces bittersweet chocolate, finely chopped

sharp cheddar cheese, shredded, for serving

scallions, white and green parts, chopped, for serving

1. Heat the oil in a large saucepan over medium heat. Add the ground turkey and cook, stirring occasionally and breaking up the meat with the side of a spoon, until its liquid has evaporated and the turkey begins to brown, about 12 minutes.

2. Add the onions and garlic and cook, stirring occasionally, until softened, about 5 minutes. Stir in the chili powder, cumin, and oregano, followed by the tomatoes with their juices, broth, lager, and tomato paste. Season with salt and pepper. Bring to a boil. Reduce the heat to medium low and partially cover the saucepan. Simmer, stirring occasionally, to blend the flavors, about 20 minutes. Stir in the beans and cook until the cooking juices are thickened, about 10 minutes more. Stir in the chocolate until it is melted.

3. Spoon the chili into bowls and sprinkle the cheese and scallions on top. Serve hot.

turkey meatballs in smoky tomato-cumin sauce

Meatballs have always been a favorite comfort food of mine. I use ground turkey breast instead of beef, and my tomato sauce includes this Latina's favorite seasonings—cumin and smoky chipotle chiles in adobo. Four chipotles make the dish nice and spicy, but use fewer if you wish. Serve over whole-wheat spaghetti, polenta, or Israeli couscous.

MAKES 4 TO 6 SERVINGS

meatballs:

1 pound ground turkey breast

⅓ cup plain dry bread crumbs

2 tablespoons fresh cilantro, finely chopped

1 teaspoon ground cumin

½ teaspoon kosher salt

¼ teaspoon freshly ground black pepper

¾ cup onion, shredded (use the large holes on a box grater)

2 teaspoons minced garlic

2 large eggs, slightly beaten

sauce:

1 28-ounce can tomato puree

1½ cups shredded onion (use the large holes on a box shredder)

1 cup chicken broth

2 teaspoons ground cumin

1 tablespoon plus 1½ teaspoons dried oregano

4 chipotle chiles in adobo sauce, seeded and minced

2 whole garlic cloves, crushed under a knife and peeled

2 tablespoons olive oil

fresh cilantro, chopped, for garnish (optional)

1. To prepare the meatballs, using your hands, combine the ingredients in a large bowl. Shape 24 meatballs from the mixture. Place on a platter, cover, and refrigerate until ready to cook.

2. To make the sauce, puree the tomato puree, onion, broth, cumin, oregano, chipotles with their adobo, and garlic in a blender.

3. Heat the oil in a large Dutch oven over medium heat. In batches, add the meatballs and cook, turning occasionally, until lightly browned, about 4 minutes. Using a slotted spoon, transfer the meatballs to a plate. Add the chipotle puree to the Dutch oven and partially cover the pot. Bring to a simmer. Reduce the heat to medium-low and simmer, stirring occasionally, to blend the flavors, about 10 minutes. Return the meatballs to the Dutch oven and stir gently to coat with the sauce. Cover completely and simmer, stirring halfway through cooking, until the meatballs are opaque when pierced with the tip of a knife, about 15 minutes.

4. Transfer to a serving bowl, sprinkle with the cilantro, if using, and serve hot.

Indulge!
latin-style fried chicken
(chicharrones de pollo)

If you love fried chicken as much as I do, you know that we can enjoy it only as an occasional indulgence. If I'm going to make—and eat—fried chicken, then it had better be worth it. And this Dominican-style fried chicken recipe is.

MAKES 4 SERVINGS

marinated chicken:

1 cup fresh lime juice

4 garlic cloves, chopped

1 tablespoon soy sauce

1 teaspoon dried oregano

8 chicken breast halves, thighs, or a combination, with skin and bones

seasoning:

1 cup all-purpose flour

1 teaspoon sweet paprika

1½ teaspoons kosher salt

½ teaspoon freshly ground black pepper

2 cups peanut oil

1. To marinate the chicken, combine the lime juice, garlic, soy sauce, and oregano in a large zip-tight plastic bag. Add the chicken and mix to coat. Close the bag and refrigerate, turning the bag occasionally, for 2 to 3 hours.

2. Drain the chicken and pat it dry with paper towels. Combine the flour, paprika, salt, and pepper in a shallow bowl. In batches, dredge the chicken in the flour mixture and shake off the excess. Transfer to a plate.

3. Heat the oil in a large, deep skillet over medium-high heat until it registers 355°F on a deep-frying thermometer.

4. In batches without crowding, add the chicken to the oil. Fry, turning the chicken occasionally, until golden brown and an Instant Read Thermometer inserted in the thickest part of the chicken registers 165°F, 12 to 14 minutes (remove the chicken from the oil for testing). Transfer to a wire cake rack placed over a baking sheet or paper towels to drain and cool slightly. Serve hot.

mac chica swanish
(grilled chicken sandwich with special sauce)

When I was little I couldn't pronounce the word "sandwich," but said "swanish" instead. A swanish could be anything from a tuna sandwich to a fast-food burger. As an adult, I find myself craving a fast-food burger every once in a while. I decided to create a sandwich with those same flavors for the occasional indulgence. Kids of all ages will love these.

MAKES 4 SERVINGS

sauce:

½ cup mayonnaise

2 tablespoons plus 1½ teaspoons creamy French dressing

2 tablespoons sweet pickle relish

2 tablespoons minced white onion

1 teaspoon distilled white vinegar

1 teaspoon sugar

kosher salt, to taste

freshly ground black pepper, to taste

sandwich:

4 boneless, skinless thin-sliced chicken breast cutlets

2 teaspoons Delicioso Adobo Seasoning (page 8)

1 tablespoon Worcestershire sauce

cooking spray

8 thin sharp cheddar cheese slices

4 6-inch oblong sandwich rolls, split lengthwise

2 cups iceberg lettuce, finely shredded

1 ripe Hass avocado, pitted, peeled, and sliced

dill pickles, sliced

1. To make the sauce, mix the ingredients in a small bowl. Cover with plastic wrap and refrigerate for at least 1 hour to blend the flavors.

2. On a plate, season the chicken cutlets on both sides with the adobo and Worcestershire sauce.

3. Spray a large grill pan with cooking spray and heat over medium-high heat. Add the chicken cutlets and cook until the underside is seared with grill marks and opaque, 3 to 4 minutes. Flip the chicken and top with the cheese. Cook until the undersides are seared and opaque and the cheese is melted, about 3 minutes more. Transfer to a platter.

4. Place the rolls, cut sides down, in the grill pan and cook until lightly toasted, about 1 minute. Spread each roll with some of the sauce, and add a chicken cutlet, ¼ of the lettuce and avocado, and some pickles. Close the roll, cut in half diagonally, and serve.

chipotle-rum-orange-pork chops

carne knowledge

I'm a meat lover who enjoys a great piece of steak, a veal chop, or pork stew now and then. I say now and then because meat, just like chocolate, cheese, and wine, is best enjoyed in moderation. When I do eat meat, I find that a sensible portion of four to six ounces is plenty. Also, meat is so filling and satisfying, it keeps me from eating too much of everything else. I use leaner cuts of meat—pork tenderloin instead of shoulder—when possible, but the fattier, inexpensive cuts, such as brisket, are flavorful and tender when cooked. Trim off as much excess fat as possible before cooking. With these preparations, I can now have my meat and eat it, too.

mango *mojo* pork

Mojo is popular throughout the Caribbean, but most notably in Cuba. Chunks of pork—I use whole pork tenderloins—are marinated in a sweet-and-sour mixture, then dusted with a gutsy peppercorn–star anise spice rub. Seared and then roasted, the pork can be served hot or at room temperature, making this dish a great buffet table addition.

marinade:

1 tablespoon vegetable oil

1 tablespoon annatto seeds (achiote)

1 mango, pitted, peeled, and cut into 1-inch pieces

¾ cup fresh orange juice

½ cup fresh lime juice

½ small red onion, thinly sliced

3 garlic cloves, coarsely chopped

1 tablespoon honey

1½ pounds pork tenderloins, silverskin and excess fat removed, cut into 3-inch pieces

spice rub:

4 star anise

2 tablespoons light brown sugar

¾ teaspoon black peppercorns

¾ teaspoon salt

1 tablespoon canola oil

1 teaspoon unsalted butter

mango topping:

1 mango, pitted, peeled and cut into ½-inch dice

1 medium yellow onion, chopped

½ cup fresh cilantro, chopped

1. To make the marinade, heat the oil in a small skillet over medium heat. Add the annatto seeds and cook, stirring almost constantly, until the oil turns golden, 2 to 3 minutes. Strain the oil and discard the seeds.

2. Pulse the mango, orange juice, lime juice, onion, garlic, honey, and annatto oil in a food processor or blender until smooth. Pour the marinade in a large zip-tight plastic bag. Add the pork. Squeeze out the air and seal the bag. Refrigerate, turning the bag occasionally, at least 2 hours or overnight.

3. Meanwhile, to make the rub, finely grind the star anise, brown sugar, peppercorns, and salt in an electric spice grinder.

4. Remove the pork from the marinade and discard the marinade. Scrape the excess marinade off the pork. Pat the pork dry with paper towels. Transfer the pork to a large bowl. Add the spice mixture and toss until well coated.

5. Preheat the oven to 400°F.

6. Heat the oil and butter in a large ovenproof skillet over medium-high heat. Add the pork and cook until browned on all sides, about 5 minutes. Transfer the skillet to the oven and cook until the pork looks opaque when pierced with the tip of a sharp knife, about 10 minutes. Transfer the pork to a platter.

7. To make the topping, toss the mango, onion, and cilantro in a medium bowl. Spoon over the pork and serve hot.

mexican pork *pozole*

Pozole is a thick, hominy-based stew usually made with pork shoulder, but I use leaner loin, which has far less fat. Bowls of shredded cabbage, sliced avocado, radishes, chopped cilantro, and lime wedges are set on the table so each person can flavor the *pozole* as they wish. Serve this warming and hearty *pozole* with some tortillas and Mexican beer.

4 dried whole New Mexico chiles

1 cup boiling water

2 teaspoons peanut oil

8 ounces boneless pork loin chops, trimmed and cut into ½-inch pieces

1 medium yellow onion, chopped

6 garlic cloves, finely chopped

2 teaspoons dried Mexican oregano

4 cups reduced-sodium chicken broth

2 15.5-ounce cans white hominy, drained and rinsed

kosher salt

½ cup green cabbage, shredded

1 Hass avocado, pitted, peeled, and thinly sliced

¼ cup radishes, thinly sliced

¼ cup fresh cilantro, chopped

2 limes, quartered

1. Place the chiles in a heatproof medium bowl. Pour the boiling water over the chiles. Let stand until soft, about 30 minutes. Drain, reserving ¼ cup of the liquid. Cut the chiles lengthwise in half and discard the stems and seeds. Transfer to a blender or food processor and puree with the reserved liquid. Transfer to a bowl and set aside.

2. Meanwhile, heat 1 teaspoon oil in a Dutch oven over medium-high heat. Add the pork and cook, turning occasionally, until browned, about 5 minutes. Transfer the pork to a plate.

3. Add the remaining 1 teaspoon oil, onion, and garlic to the Dutch oven. Cook over medium-high heat, stirring occasionally, until the onion is softened, about 5 minutes. Stir in the chile paste and oregano and mix well.

4. Return the pork to the Dutch oven. Add the broth and hominy and bring to a boil. Reduce the heat to medium low and cover. Simmer, stirring occasionally, until the flavors are blended and the *pozole* thickens slightly, about 1 hour. Season with salt.

5. To serve, ladle the *pozole* into soup bowls. Allow each guest to top with cabbage, avocado, radishes, and cilantro, as desired, and serve lime wedges on the side for squeezing.

yucatán-style pulled pork
(*cochinita pibil*)

On Mexico's Yucatán peninsula, pork shoulder is marinated in achiote paste, orange juice, and lime and then wrapped in a banana leaf and slow roasted. The acidic marinade and slow cooking time tenderize the meat and impart a vibrant orange color and sweet-peppery flavor.

Pork shoulder, called *pernil* at Latin markets, is an inexpensive cut, but it is very large, so ask for a half-roast. Boston butt pork roast also works well. Frozen banana leaves are used to wrap the pork, hold in the moisture, and help tenderize the meat. They can be found at Latin and Asian markets. If you can't find banana leaves, wrap the marinated roast in aluminum foil.

MAKES 6 SERVINGS

pork:

1 tablespoon annatto seeds

1 tablespoon dried oregano

1 teaspoon kosher salt

½ teaspoon ground cumin

5 black peppercorns

4 whole allspice berries

4 whole cloves

¼ cup fresh cilantro, finely chopped

5 garlic cloves, chopped (about 2½ tablespoons)

2 habanero chiles, seeded and finely chopped

½ cup fresh orange juice

⅓ cup distilled white vinegar

¼ cup fresh lime juice

1 4-pound bone-in, skinless pork shoulder (picnic) or Boston butt roast

pickled onions:

1 red onion, halved and sliced in ⅛-inch-thick half-moons (about 3 cups)

½ cup chopped fresh cilantro

1 habanero chile, deveined, seeded, and finely chopped

kosher salt

freshly ground black pepper

1 cup distilled white vinegar

¼ cup fresh lime juice

2 banana leaves

1. To prepare the pork, process the annatto, dried oregano, salt, cumin, peppercorns, allspice, and cloves together in a spice grinder or clean coffee grinder into a finely ground powder. Transfer to a small bowl. Add the cilantro, garlic, and chiles and stir to form a paste.

2. In a large bowl, combine orange juice, vinegar, and lime juice. Using a wooden skewer, pierce the pork shoulder on all sides. Coat the pork on all sides with the reserved spice mixture, rubbing it into the meat. Place the pork in the juice mixture; cover and refrigerate, turning the pork halfway through the marinating time, for at least 2 hours and up to 12 hours.

3. Meanwhile, make the pickled onions. Combine the onions, cilantro, and chile in a large bowl, and season with salt and pepper. Pour in the vinegar and lime juice and stir well. Cover the bowl and refrigerate at least 6 hours and up to 8 hours.

4. Remove the pork from the refrigerator and let stand at room temperature for 30 minutes to lose its chill.

5. Preheat the oven to 300°F.

6. Line the bottom and sides of a Dutch oven with long pieces of aluminum foil, letting the foil overhang the sides of the pot by 6 inches. Fit 1 banana leaf, running lengthwise, in the Dutch oven, pressing the leaf to fit the pot, and letting the ends of the leaf overhang the edges of the pot. Repeat with a second banana leaf, running crosswise.

7. Remove the pork from the marinade and put in the pot. Pour in the marinade. Fold the overhanging leaves over entirely to cover the pork. Fold the aluminum foil "tails" toward the center and over the leaves, making sure they are securely enclosed. Cover the Dutch oven with a well-fitting lid to ensure that no moisture escapes. Bake for 4 hours, until the pork is very tender. Serve hot.

pork and chicken paella

This version of the signature rice dish from Spain is called *mixta*, or mixed paella, because it has both pork and chicken. The *sofrito* of slowly cooked peppers, onion, and garlic is the building block of many Spanish dishes. No need to purchase a special pan to make paella. A twelve-inch skillet will do. This can be made up to four hours in advance and covered with aluminum foil. When ready to reheat, set the skillet on top of a pot of boiling water for 8 to 10 minutes (the pot should be large enough for the skillet to sit snugly on top of it). The steam will heat the paella without drying out the rice and other ingredients.

MAKES 4 TO 6 SERVINGS

2 tablespoons olive oil

1 pound boneless, skinless chicken thighs, excess fat removed, cut into 2-inch pieces

1 pound baby back ribs, cut into ribs, then chopped across the bone into 1-inch pieces

6 ounces hard Spanish-style chorizo, thinly sliced

1 medium red bell pepper, cored, seeded, and ribbed, cut into thin strips

1 medium green bell pepper, cored, seeded, and ribbed, cut into thin strips

1 medium yellow onion, chopped

4 garlic cloves, finely chopped

1 cup long-grain brown rice

1 10-ounce can diced tomatoes with chiles

3 tablespoons tomato paste

1 teaspoon saffron threads, crumbled

2½ cups reduced-sodium chicken broth

½ cup frozen peas, thawed

⅓ cup fresh flat-leaf parsley leaves, finely chopped

kosher salt

freshly ground black pepper

1 lemon, cut into 6 wedges

1. Heat 1 tablespoon of oil in a large nonstick skillet or paella pan over medium-high heat. In batches, add the chicken and ribs and cook, turning occasionally, until browned, about 8 minutes. Transfer to a large bowl.

2. Add the chorizo, red and green bell peppers, onion, and garlic and cook, stirring occasionally, until the onion softens, about 6 minutes. Add the rice, diced tomatoes, tomato paste, and saffron to the skillet and mix well. Return the chicken and ribs and cook, stirring occasionally, about 5 minutes. Meanwhile, bring the broth to a boil in a medium saucepan. In five or six additions, stir the boiling stock into the rice, cooking and stirring until the broth is almost completely absorbed before adding more, until you get to the final addition.

3. Reduce the heat to low and cover tightly. Simmer until the rice is tender and the liquid is absorbed, about 45 minutes. Stir in the peas and parsley and cook until the peas are heated through, about 1 minute. Season with salt and pepper. Serve hot with the lemon wedges.

chipotle-rum-orange pork chops

For a quick midweek family dinner, I brown some pork chops in a skillet, brush them with a glaze, and then finish them in the oven. Serve the chops with some Jicama Slaw (page 96) and Yellow Pepper Quinoa (page 231).

(page 96)
(page 231)

MAKES 4 SERVINGS

4 center-cut pork loin chops, with bone, cut 1 inch thick

kosher salt

freshly ground black pepper

4 teaspoons olive oil

freshly grated zest of 2 oranges

⅔ cup fresh orange juice

1 canned chipotle pepper in adobo, minced, with 1 teaspoon adobo sauce

¼ cup dark rum

3 tablespoons honey

¼ teaspoon garlic powder

⅛ teaspoon ground allspice

orange slices, for garnish

1. Season the pork with 1½ teaspoons salt and 1 teaspoon pepper. Heat a large skillet over medium-high heat until very hot. Add the oil and heat until shimmering but not smoking, about 30 seconds. In batches, if necessary, add the pork and cook, turning as needed, until browned on both sides, about 10 minutes. Transfer to a plate.

2. Add the orange zest, orange juice, chipotle, rum, honey, garlic powder, and allspice and bring to a boil, scraping up the browned bits in the skillet with a wooden spoon. Return the pork to the skillet. Reduce the heat to medium low. Simmer, stirring occasionally, until the sauce is lightly thickened and the pork looks opaque when pierced in the thickest part with the tip of a sharp knife, 8 to 10 minutes. Season with salt and pepper.

3. Transfer the pork to a platter and pour the sauce on top. Garnish with the orange slices and serve hot.

bolivian fricassee with baby back ribs and hominy (*fritanga boliviana*)

Fritanga, a spicy pork stew, is a traditional one-pot Bolivian dish. Cooked slowly, baby back ribs become falling-off-the-bone tender. Simmered for hours with garlic, mint, and cumin, thickened with hominy and potatoes, the pork shreds at the slightest touch of a fork. I have fond memories of my grandfather making this for us when I was a child.

6 teaspoons olive oil

2 pounds baby back ribs, cut into single ribs

2 large tomatoes, diced (about 4 cups)

2 cups yellow onion, chopped

2 tablespoons fresh flat-leaf parsley leaves, chopped

1 tablespoon fresh mint leaves, chopped

1 tablespoon ground chili powder

1¾ teaspoons kosher salt

1 teaspoon ground cumin

1 teaspoon dried oregano

½ teaspoon freshly ground black pepper

8 cups water

3 medium baking potatoes, such as russet, peeled, halved lengthwise, and cut into ¼-inch-thick slices

1 15.5-ounce can white hominy, drained and rinsed

1. Heat 2 teaspoons of the oil in a large skillet over medium-high heat. Add 4 ribs. Cook, turning after 2 minutes, until golden brown, about 4 minutes. Transfer to a plate. Repeat twice with the remaining oil and ribs.

2. Stir the tomato, onion, parsley, mint, chili powder, salt, cumin, oregano, and pepper together in a Dutch oven. Add the reserved ribs to the pot along with any cooking juices in the skillet. Mix well and add 8 cups of water. Bring to a boil over medium-high heat. Lower the heat and simmer, partially covered, until the meat is tender, about 1 hour. Add the potatoes and cook until they are just tender, about 15 minutes. Remove from the heat.

3. Transfer 3 cups of the broth from the pot to a blender. Using a slotted spoon, transfer 10 potato slices. Place a kitchen towel, not the lid, over the blender to allow steam to escape. Blend until smooth. Return blended mixture to the pot and stir to combine.

4. Bring a saucepan of water to a boil over medium-high heat. Add the hominy and cook just until heated through, about 3 minutes. Drain well.

5. Divide the hominy evenly among 6 large, shallow bowls. Top each with equal amounts of the stew and serve hot.

spanish hazelnut and parsley veal chops

Veal is a delicate meat that requires careful cooking and close attention. My favorite way to cook veal chops is to sear them quickly, remove them to a platter, make and puree a pan sauce, and then roast everything in the oven. This hazelnut-parsley sauce won't overpower the veal. For a simple but elegant dinner, serve with Rosemary Butter Beans (page 226), Frisée Salad with Figs, Hazelnuts, and Manchego with Guava Vinaigrette (page 100), and a bottle of Tempranillo.

MAKES 4 SERVINGS

4 veal rib chops, cut 1 inch thick

kosher salt

freshly ground black pepper

1 tablespoons olive oil

1 cup reduced-sodium chicken broth

2 tablespoons cider vinegar

1 small yellow onion, chopped

1 cup hazelnuts, toasted, skinned, and coarsely chopped (page 10)

2 tablespoons fresh flat-leaf parsley leaves, finely chopped, and more for serving

2 tablespoons fresh tarragon leaves, finely chopped, or 1 tablespoon dry tarragon

1. Preheat the oven to 350°F.

2. Season the veal with 1½ teaspoons salt and 1 teaspoon pepper. Heat a large ovenproof skillet over medium-high heat until very hot. Add the oil and heat until shimmering but not smoking, about 30 seconds. In batches, if necessary, add the veal and cook, turning occasionally, until golden brown on both sides, about 10 minutes. Transfer to a plate.

3. Add 2 tablespoons of broth and the vinegar to the skillet and bring to a boil, scraping up the browned bits with a wooden spoon. Add the onion and cook, stirring often, until translucent, about 2 minutes. Add the hazelnuts and cook, stirring often, to blend the flavors for 2 minutes. Stir in the remaining broth with the parsley and tarragon. Return the veal chops to the skillet. bake, uncovered, until an Instant Read Thermometer inserted horizontally through the side of a chop registers 150°F, about 15 minutes. The meat's temperature will continue to rise.

4. Remove the skillet from the oven and transfer the chops to a platter. Puree the hazelnut mixture with the pan juices in a food processor. Season with salt and pepper.

5. Divide the hazelnut sauce evenly among 4 dinner plates. Top each with a chop. Garnish with parsley and serve hot.

spicy *pepita* beef stew

Sauces made with seeds and/or nuts—moles, romesco, picada—are found throughout Latin cuisine, as in this beef stew with *pepitas*, or green pumpkin seeds, and peanuts added for texture. While the stew cooks in the pressure cooker, the sauce quickly comes together in a blender. Serve with Simple Brown Rice 101 (page 234).

MAKES 4 SERVINGS

1 tablespoon vegetable oil

2 pounds boneless beef bottom round, trimmed and cut into 1½-inch chunks

2 cups reduced-sodium beef broth

1 medium yellow onion, quartered

2 teaspoons Delicioso Adobo Seasoning (page 8)

1 garlic clove, minced

1 large tomato, chopped

½ cup toasted pumpkin seeds (*pepitas*)

¼ cup dry-roasted peanuts

2 whole chipotle chiles in adobo, minced

kosher salt

1 cup fresh cilantro, coarsely chopped

2 tablespoons scallions, chopped

1. Heat the oil in a pressure cooker over medium-high heat. In batches, add the beef and cook, stirring occasionally, until browned, about 8 minutes. Transfer to a plate.

2. Return the beef to the pressure cooker. Add the broth, onion, adobo seasoning, and garlic. Lock the lid in place and increase the heat to high. Bring the cooker to high pressure. Reduce the heat to medium low and maintain the pressure for 15 minutes.

3. Place the pot in a sink and run cold water over the lid (but not the valve) to bring pressure down quickly. When the pressure indicator releases, remove the pot from the sink and unlock the lid.

4. Using a slotted spoon, transfer the meat to a serving bowl and cover with aluminum foil to keep warm. Pour the cooking liquid into a blender and add the tomato, *pepitas*, peanuts, and chipotles. With the lid ajar, puree the mixture, and return to the pressure cooker. Simmer uncovered over medium-low heat, stirring often, until the sauce begins to thicken, about 10 minutes. Season with salt. Pour the sauce over the beef, sprinkle with the cilantro and scallions, and serve hot.

carne knowledge

tequila drunken fajitas

These festive steak fajitas aren't just meaty and smoky—they sizzle with broiled bell peppers, scallions, and an eye-opening tequila-orange marinade. Skirt steak, lean and thin, is my absolute favorite cut of meat with its intense beefy flavor. The tough cut of meat takes to bracing marinades very well, resulting in tender strips of steak.

marinade:

2 pounds skirt or flank steak

4 garlic cloves, finely minced

3 tablespoons tequila, preferably gold tequila

2 tablespoons fresh lime juice

2 tablespoons fresh orange juice

freshly grated zest of ¼ orange

2 tablespoons red wine vinegar

1 teaspoon light or dark brown sugar

½ teaspoon freshly ground black pepper

¼ teaspoon red pepper flakes

¼ cup olive oil

3 tablespoons fresh cilantro, chopped

16 scallions, white and light green part only

2 red bell peppers, cored, seeded, ribbed, and sliced

2 tablespoons olive oil

1 teaspoon dried oregano

kosher salt

8 8-inch whole-wheat or multigrain tortillas, heated

2 ripe Hass avocados, halved, pitted, peeled, and thinly sliced

fresh cilantro, chopped, for serving

lime wedges, for serving

hot sauce, for serving

1. Place the steak in a shallow baking dish and rub it with the garlic. Whisk the tequila, lime and orange juices, orange zest, vinegar, brown sugar, pepper, and red pepper flakes in a small bowl. Whisk in the oil and pour over the meat. Press 1½ tablespoons of cilantro onto each side of the steak in an even layer. Cover the baking dish with plastic wrap and refrigerate, turning the steak occasionally, for at least 4 hours or overnight.

2. Position the broiler rack about 6 inches from the source of heat and preheat the broiler. Toss the scallions and red peppers in a bowl with the olive oil and oregano and season with salt.

3. Remove the steak from the marinade and season with salt. Place the steak, scallions, and peppers on an aluminum foil–lined baking sheet or the broiler pan. Broil, flipping the steak after 5 minutes, until browned on both sides and the meat feels soft with some resilience when pressed on top in the center, about 10 minutes for medium rare (slightly longer for flank steak). Broil the scallions and peppers, turning occasionally, until softened and browned, about 8 minutes. Transfer the steak to a cutting board, cover loosely with aluminum foil and let it rest for 5 minutes. Transfer the scallions and peppers to a serving bowl.

4. Meanwhile, heat a medium skillet over medium-high heat. One at a time, add a tortilla and heat, flipping once, until pliable and heated through, 30 to 45 seconds. Transfer to a plate and cover with a kitchen towel to keep warm. (Alternatively, stack the tortillas on a plate, cover with a damp cloth, and microwave on high for 30 seconds and keep them covered until you're ready to serve.)

5. Cut the steak into thin slices against the grain and serve with the warm tortillas, the scallions, peppers and some avocado slices. Pass the remaining cilantro, lime wedges, and your favorite hot sauce to season to taste.

carne knowledge

mexican meat loaf with tequila ketchup

When I'm feeling nostalgic and craving Mom's good old-fashioned meat loaf, this is my go-to recipe. It's comfort food at its best.

cooking spray

tequila ketchup:

1 cup organic ketchup

2 tablespoons apple cider vinegar

1 tablespoon tequila

1 teaspoon Worcestershire sauce

¼ teaspoon chipotle powder

meat loaf:

1 tablespoon olive oil

1 onion, finely chopped

2 carrots, grated (about ¾ cup)

2 garlic cloves, minced

1 teaspoon chili powder

½ teaspoon chipotle powder

½ teaspoon ground cumin

1 teaspoon Worcestershire sauce

1 cup chopped fresh cilantro

1 pound lean ground beef

1 pound ground turkey breast

2 large eggs

½ cup plain dry bread crumbs

¾ teaspoon salt

1. Preheat the oven to 350°F. Line a rimmed baking sheet with foil; spray the foil with cooking spray.

2. To make the Tequila Ketchup, combine the ketchup, vinegar, tequila, Worcestershire sauce, and chipotle powder in a small bowl until blended. Set aside.

3. To make the meat loaf, heat the oil in a large nonstick skillet over medium-high heat. Add the onion, carrot, garlic, chili powder, chipotle powder, cumin, and Worcestershire sauce. Cook, stirring occasionally, until the vegetables are tender, about 8 minutes. Remove from the heat; stir in the cilantro. Transfer to a large bowl and let cool slightly. Add the beef, turkey, eggs, bread crumbs, salt, and ½ cup of the ketchup mixture, mixing lightly just until blended.

4. Transfer the mixture to the baking sheet and form into a 6 × 9-inch loaf. Spread the remaining ketchup mixture over the top of the loaf. Bake until an Instant Read Thermometer inserted into the center of the loaf registers 160°F, about 1 hour and 10 minutes. Let stand 5 minutes before slicing.

peruvian *anticucho* beef skewers

Anticuchos, grilled skewers of meat, are a street food popular in the Andean regions of Peru and Bolivia, where they're traditionally made with beef hearts. I marinate cubes of beef in a sauce made with lots of garlic and some *ají panca*, a mild chile paste from Peru.

MAKES 8 TO 10 SERVINGS

¼ cup mild *ají panca* paste

¼ cup distilled white vinegar

12 garlic cloves, minced

1 tablespoon ground cumin

1 teaspoon dried oregano

1 teaspoon kosher salt

½ teaspoon freshly ground black pepper

2½ pounds sirloin steak, cut into 2 x 1-inch cubes

10 metal grilling skewers, or use bamboo skewers, soaked in water for 30 minutes, drained

nonstick olive oil cooking spray

1. Mix the *ají panca* paste, vinegar, garlic, cumin, oregano, salt, and pepper in a large bowl.

2. Put the beef in a large zip-tight plastic bag and pour in the vinegar mixture. Squeeze out the air and close the bag. Refrigerate, turning occasionally, for at least 8 hours and up to 16 hours. (Or, if you are pressed for time, marinate the beef at room temperature for 1 hour.)

3. Prepare an outdoor grill or preheat a grill pan over medium-high heat.

4. Thread equal amounts of the beef onto the skewers. Spray the skewers with cooking spray.

5. If grilling, brush the grill grates clean. If using a grill pan, you will have to grill the skewers in batches. Grill or pan-grill the skewers, turning occasionally, until browned, about 8 minutes for medium rare. Transfer to a platter and serve immediately.

argentine stuffed rolled flank steak
(*matahambre*)

Matahambre means "hunger killer" in Spanish. I'll say! This is some hearty dish. Before filling a butterflied flank steak with vegetables, hard-cooked eggs, and other ingredients, I marinate the meat in milk so it's tender and juicy. The flank steak is rolled up, tied, and seared before being braised in wine, broth, and herbs.

1 2½-pound flank steak, trimmed of excess fat

kosher salt

freshly ground black pepper

1 cup milk

2 cups Swiss chard leaves, well rinsed and coarsely chopped

2 carrots, shredded

3 large hard-cooked eggs, peeled and quartered lengthwise

½ cup large pitted green Spanish olives, halved lengthwise

½ small yellow onion, sliced into thin rings

⅓ cup small pickled hot peppers, such as Goya, drained and chopped

¼ cup freshly grated Parmesan cheese

1 tablespoon olive oil

1 cup hearty red wine, preferably Argentine malbec

1 cup reduced-sodium beef broth

1 large yellow onion, cut into 4 wedges

¼ cup fresh flat-leaf parsley, chopped

1 head garlic, cut in half

6 fresh thyme sprigs

6 fresh oregano sprigs

2 bay leaves

3 tablespoons all-purpose flour

¼ cup water

1. Place the steak on a cutting board with the grain running toward you. Holding a thin sharp knife parallel to the board and starting at one long side, butterfly the steak: Cut with the grain almost to the other side, and open up the steak like a book. Place a piece of plastic wrap over the meat. Gently pound with a meat mallet or rolling pin until the meat is evenly thick. Season with ½ teaspoon salt and ¼ teaspoon pepper. Place the meat in a small shallow baking dish and pour in the milk. Cover with plastic wrap and refrigerate for 4 hours or overnight.

2. Pour off the milk and pat the steak dry with paper towels. Place the meat on a work surface. Scatter the Swiss chard evenly over the top, leaving a 1-inch border. Sprinkle the carrots evenly over the Swiss chard. Top evenly with the eggs, olives, onion slices, pickled peppers, and cheese. From a short side, carefully roll up the meat jelly roll style. Tie with kitchen string at 1-inch intervals.

3. Heat the oil in a Dutch oven over medium-high heat. Add the meat roulade and cook, turning occasionally, until browned on all sides, about 5 minutes. Add the wine, broth, onion wedges, parsley, garlic, thyme, oregano, and bay leaves and bring to a boil. Reduce the heat to me-

dium low and cover. Simmer until the meat is fork tender, about 1½ hours.

4. Transfer the meat to a cutting board. Tent with aluminum foil and let stand for 15 minutes.

5. With a slotted spoon, remove and discard the garlic, herb stems, and bay leaves from the cooking liquid. Bring to a simmer. Whisk together the flour and water in a small bowl until smooth. Gradually whisk the flour mixture into the simmering liquid, and return to a simmer. Cook, whisking often, until the sauce has no raw flour taste, 3 to 4 minutes. Season with salt and pepper. Pour into a large sauceboat.

6. Remove the strings and cut the roulade crosswise into ½-inch-thick slices. Serve the *matahambre* with the sauce.

colombian-style tri-tip *posta negra*

Inexpensive and easy, this classic from the Colombian coast goes well with Caramelized Onions and Lentil Rice (page 225) and Classic Latin Avocado and Tomato Salad (page 101).

1 garlic head

1 tablespoon kosher salt

2 tablespoons olive oil

4 pounds tri-tip roast or *picanha*

2 medium red onions, sliced

4 medium tomatoes, sliced

½ cup soy sauce

1. Preheat the oven to 375°F.

2. Coarsely chop the garlic on a chopping board. Sprinkle with some of the salt and continue chopping and smearing the garlic on the board to make a garlic paste. Transfer to a small bowl and stir in the remaining salt. Rub all over the meat and let stand for 5 minutes.

3. Heat the oil in a large ovenproof skillet over medium-high heat until the oil is shimmering but not smoking. Add the meat and cook, turning occasionally, just until the garlic begins to brown, about 6 minutes. Transfer the skillet to the oven and bake until an Instant Read Thermometer inserted in the thickest part of the meat registers 140°F, about 35 minutes. Transfer to a carving board and let stand for 10 minutes. (This period allows the juices to redistribute throughout the meat and will help keep the meat juicy.)

4. Meanwhile, discard all but 1 tablespoon of the fat in the skillet. Heat over medium heat and add the onions and tomatoes. Cook, stirring occasionally, until the vegetables are tender, about 10 minutes. Transfer to a food processor and pulse just until coarsely chopped. Transfer the sauce to a serving bowl and stir in the soy sauce.

5. Slice the beef against the grain and transfer to a platter. Pour the sauce over the beef and serve immediately.

carne knowledge

pork-apricot fried rice

I never order fried rice in restaurants because it's usually greasy, salty, and bland. And it's so easy to make at home. A hot—really hot—skillet is the secret. I like to add some dried apricots and pineapple juice for a touch of sweetness.

MAKES 6 SERVINGS

rice:

1 tablespoon vegetable oil

2 cups long-grain rice

2 cups unsweetened pineapple juice

2 cups water

⅓ cup dried apricots, sliced

2 teaspoons kosher salt

pork:

1½ tablespoons peanut oil

1½ pounds boneless pork loin, cut into ¼-inch chunks

1½ teaspoons kosher salt

½ teaspoon freshly ground black pepper

2 garlic cloves, chopped

½ cup fresh cilantro, chopped

¼ cup celery, finely chopped

¼ cup scallions, white and green parts, finely chopped

2 tablespoons reduced-sodium soy sauce

2 teaspoons sherry wine vinegar

1 tablespoon fresh ginger, finely grated

¼ cup pistachios, toasted, for garnish

1. For the rice, heat the oil in a large saucepan over medium heat. Add the rice and cook, stirring often, until the rice looks chalky, about 2 minutes. Add the pineapple juice, water, apricots, and salt and bring to a boil. Cook until the liquid is below the surface of the rice and tunnels form in the rice. Reduce the heat to low and cover. Cook until the rice is tender, 15 to 20 minutes.

2. For the pork, heat the oil in a Dutch oven over medium-high heat. Season the pork with the salt and pepper. In batches, add to the skillet and cook, turning occasionally, until lightly browned, about 7 minutes. Transfer to a plate. Return the pork to the skillet. Add garlic, ¼ cup of cilantro, celery, scallions, soy sauce, sherry vinegar, and ginger. Stir-fry until the celery is tender, about 3 minutes. Add the rice and stir-fry until well mixed, 3 to 5 minutes. Sprinkle with the pistachios and the remaining cilantro and serve hot.

mexican juicy beef *(carne en su jugo)*

To describe *carne en su jugo* as a dish made with beef, bacon, and beans would be doing a great disservice to this Mexican classic. It's one of those dishes that's so much more than its individual ingredients. Briefly marinated sliced steak is cooked in bacon drippings with cilantro, scallions, chipotles, and some broth until tender. The beef is ladled into bowls over beans and accompanied by garnishes.

MAKES 4 SERVINGS

1½ pounds flank steak, cut into 1-inch pieces

⅓ cup fresh lime juice

2 tablespoons Worcestershire sauce

5 bacon strips, coarsely chopped

½ cup fresh cilantro, finely chopped

2 scallions, white and green parts, thinly sliced

2 jalapeños, seeded and minced

1 tablespoon Delicioso Abobo Seasoning (page 8)

3 cups reduced-sodium beef broth

kosher salt

freshly ground black pepper

1 15-ounce can pinto beans, not drained and rinsed

½ cup fresh cilantro, finely chopped

2 scallions, white and green parts, thinly sliced

4 radishes, thinly sliced

1 lime, cut into 4 wedges

1. Toss the flank steak with the lime juice and Worcestershire sauce in a large bowl until well coated. Let stand at room temperature for 15 minutes. Strain the steak in a colander over a bowl, saving the marinade. Pat the steak dry with paper towels.

2. Cook the bacon in a Dutch oven over medium-high heat, stirring occasionally, until browned and crisp, about 5 minutes. With a slotted spoon, transfer the bacon to paper towels to drain.

3. Discard all but 1 tablespoon of bacon fat from the Dutch oven and heat over medium-high heat. In batches, add the steak to the Dutch oven and cook, turning occasionally, until browned. Transfer to a plate.

4. Return the steak to the Dutch oven. Add the cilantro, scallions, jalapeños, and adobo seasoning. Cook, stirring occasionally, until the jalapeños soften, about 3 minutes. Add the broth, salt and pepper and bring to a boil. Reduce the heat to medium low. Simmer, stirring occasionally, until the steak is tender, about 20 minutes.

5. Meanwhile, bring the beans and their liquid to a boil in a small saucepan over medium heat. Reduce the heat to medium low and simmer until hot, about 3 minutes.

6. Divide the beans and liquid among 4 soup bowls, and top each with the stew. Serve hot, allowing guests to sprinkle their serving with cilantro, scallions, radishes, and bacon. Serve with the lime wedges for squeezing.

apple-tomatillo brisket

Brisket is just perfect for the pressure cooker; it needs to be cooked low and slow. And it cooks in about half the time it would take if you made it in the oven. The tomatillos and apples put a contemporary spin on a classic preparation.

MAKES 4 TO 6 SERVINGS

2½ pounds beef brisket

2 teaspoons Delicioso Adobo Seasoning (page 8)

2 tablespoons canola oil

7 tomatillos, husks removed, rinsed, and quartered

3 sweet, not tart, apples, such as Rome Beauty, Gala, or Honeycrisp, peeled, cored, and chopped

2 medium yellow onions, chopped

½ cup celery, chopped

½ cup carrots, chopped

¼ cup fresh cilantro, chopped, and more for serving

3 garlic cloves, chopped

2 jalapeños, seeded and minced

1 teaspoon kosher salt

¼ teaspoon ground cumin

1 bay leaf

1½ cups reduced-sodium chicken broth

1. Rub the brisket evenly with the adobo seasoning. Heat the oil in a large pressure cooker (mine is 6 quarts) over medium-high heat. Add the brisket and cook, turning once, until browned, about 6 minutes. Transfer to a plate.

2. Add the tomatillos, apples, onion, celery, carrots, cilantro, garlic, jalapeños, salt, cumin, and bay leaf. Cook, stirring occasionally, to blend the flavors, about 5 minutes. Return the brisket to the pressure cooker and pour in the broth. Lock the lid in place.

3. Bring the pressure to high over high heat. Adjust the heat to medium low to maintain high pressure. Cook for 1½ hours. Release the pressure according to the manufacturer's directions. Open the cooker and transfer the brisket to a carving board, tent with aluminum foil, and let stand for 10 minutes. In batches, puree the cooking liquid in blender with the lid ajar. Season the sauce with salt and pepper and set aside.

4. Slice the brisket against the grain and transfer to a deep platter. Spoon some of the sauce over the brisket and sprinkle with the cilantro. Serve hot, with the remaining cilantro passed on the side.

carne knowledge

latin burgers with caramelized onion and jalapeño relish and red pepper mayonnaise

If I'm going to eat a burger, it had better be worth it. So I decided to give the all-American classic an update by adding a bit of spicy chorizo and topping it with my zesty caramelized onion and jalapeño relish and a red pepper mayonnaise. When I'm asked what I'd eat for my last meal, this burger would definitely be on the menu.

MAKES 6 SERVINGS

mayonnaise:

2 medium jarred roasted red bell peppers, drained

¾ cup mayonnaise

kosher salt

freshly ground black pepper

burgers:

¾ pound ground sirloin

¾ pound ground chuck

½ pound raw Mexican chorizo, casings removed and crumbled

1 large yellow onion, grated

½ cup dried bread crumbs

1 tablespoon Delicioso Adobo Seasoning (page 8)

relish:

2 tablespoons olive oil

2 large yellow onions, halved and thinly sliced

kosher salt

freshly ground black pepper

½ cup bottled jalapeño chile slices, drained

½ cup packed dark brown sugar

2 tablespoons canola oil

6 slices Oaxaca or mozzarella cheese

6 whole-grain hamburger rolls

1. To make the red pepper mayonnaise, puree the red peppers in a blender or food processor. Add the mayonnaise and process until smooth. Season with salt and pepper. Transfer to a bowl, cover, and refrigerate for at least 4 hours or preferably overnight.

2. To prepare the burgers, thoroughly mix the ground sirloin, ground chuck, chorizo, onion, bread crumbs, and adobo seasoning in a large bowl by hand. Form the burgers into 6 patties without pressing them too much, or they can become tough. Line a baking pan with waxed paper and put the burgers side by side in a single layer. Cover and refrigerate for at least 30 minutes. This will help the burgers hold together.

3. To make the relish, heat the oil in a heavy skillet over medium-low heat. Add the onion and season with salt and pepper. Add the jalapeños and the brown sugar. Cook, stirring occasionally, until the onion and jalapeños are caramelized and tender, about 15 minutes. Transfer to a bowl and let cool.

4. To cook the burgers, preheat an outdoor grill to medium heat. Brush the grill grates clean.

carne knowledge

Lightly oil the grate. Place the burgers on the grate and cover with the grill lid. Cook, flipping the burgers every 5 minutes, until they are medium well and feel firm when pressed on top with a finger, 15 to 20 minutes (due to the raw chorizo, do not cook for less time). (Or heat a grill pan over medium-high heat. Add the burgers and cover. Cook, lowering the heat as needed, and flipping the burgers every 5 minutes, until medium well, 15 to 20 minutes.) During the last few minutes, top each burger with a cheese slice. Remove from the grill.

5. For each burger, spread about 2 tablespoons of the mayonnaise inside a roll. Add a burger and top with a couple of spoonfuls of the relish. Serve hot.

orange-basil salmon packets

ciao pescao

Growing up on an island in the Caribbean allowed me to appreciate the sea and its bounty. When I think of my biggest joys as far as spending leisure and free time, the first thing that comes to mind is definitely the ocean. Fishing is one of my hobbies and a favorite pastime. I often went fishing with my dad. I loved the thrill of catching fish, then taking them home and preparing what we caught.

For the last few years, I've been commuting between my Miami home and my boyfriend's place in Nassau, Bahamas, where we spend a lot of time fishing. Just off Nassau, there's a fishermen's paradise called the Tongue of the Ocean, one of the deepest parts of the Atlantic Ocean. We catch yellow-eye snapper and other delicacies not available commercially. These fishing trips inspire me to create fish recipes that are easy to prepare and healthy.

Fish is a great source of animal protein—probably the leanest and healthiest of all. It's rich in omega-3 fatty acids, which help prevent heart disease. I try to eat a variety of fish four to five times a week, because each one provides different nutrients, and doing so helps conserve species.

tuna and mango tacos with chipotle cream

Packed with flavor and essential omega-3 fats, tuna is a great way to add protein to your meals. This recipe is a healthful version of the battered, deep-fried fish tacos usually found on menus. A hardy fish for the grill, tuna has a meaty flavor and deep, rich color. Served in soft tortillas, the tuna gets special treatment with a lively salsa of mango, red onion, and chipotle. I always keep some of the chipotle cream in my fridge and use it on salads and sandwiches.

MAKES 4 SERVINGS

chipotle cream:

3 tablespoons fresh lemon juice

2 chipotle chiles in adobo, seeded and chopped, plus ½ teaspoon of the adobo sauce

3 garlic cloves, minced

½ teaspoon ground cumin

1 7-ounce container plain 2% fat Greek yogurt

kosher salt

freshly ground black pepper

salsa:

1 mango, peeled, fruit cut off the seed, and cut into ½-inch dice (about 1½ cups)

6 scallions, white and light green parts, thinly sliced

½ cup fresh cilantro, chopped

1 tablespoon fresh squeezed orange juice

kosher salt

freshly ground black pepper

2 ripe Hass avocados, halved, pitted, peeled, and cut into ½-inch dice

tuna:

1 tablespoon ground cumin

1 tablespoon chili powder

¼ teaspoon kosher salt

¼ teaspoon freshly ground black pepper

1 pound sushi-grade tuna steak (1½ inch thick)

1 tablespoon olive oil

4 (8-inch) whole-wheat or multigrain tortillas

1. To make the cream, process the lemon juice, chiles, garlic, and cumin together in a food processor to make a paste. Add the yogurt and pulse until thoroughly combined. Season with salt and pepper to taste.

2. To make the salsa, combine the mango, scallions, cilantro, and orange juice in a medium bowl. Season with salt and pepper. Stir well. Let stand while preparing the tuna.

3. To prepare the tuna, mix the cumin, chili powder, salt, and pepper together in a small bowl. Brush tuna with ½ tablespoon of olive oil and coat with spice mixture. Let stand for 15 minutes.

4. Meanwhile, preheat the oven to 200°F. One at a time, heat the tortillas in a dry skillet over medium heat, turning often, until warm and pliable, about 45 seconds. Stack the tortillas on a baking sheet, tent with aluminum foil, and keep warm in the oven until ready to serve.

5. Lightly brush a grill pan or cast-iron skillet with the remaining olive oil and heat over high heat. Add the tuna and cook, turning after 3 minutes, until seared on both sides, about 6 minutes for medium rare, turning once. Transfer the tuna to a carving board and let stand for 3 minutes.

Using a knife, cut against the grain into ½-inch-thick slices.

6. Gently stir the avocado into the orange mixture to finish the salsa. If you wish, transfer the cream to a plastic condiment dispenser. For each taco, put a tortilla on a plate and arrange slices of tuna over one half of it. Top with 3 generous tablespoons of salsa and squirt or spoon cream liberally over the salsa. Fold in half and serve hot.

baked costa rican–style tilapia with pineapples, black beans, and rice

To me, Costa Rica means ocean, wilderness, and *gallo pinto*, a national favorite. *Gallo pinto* means "spotted rooster," because the beans look like spots in the white rice. For this one-pot meal, the fish is marinated in orange juice and then baked on a bed of white rice, black beans, tomatoes, and pineapple.

MAKES 4 SERVINGS

1 cup long-grain white rice

2 cups low-sodium chicken broth

¼ cup fresh orange juice

2 tablespoons fresh lime juice

2 tablespoons olive oil

¼ cup fresh cilantro, plus more for garnish, finely chopped

2 garlic cloves, minced

1 teaspoon sugar

kosher salt

freshly ground black pepper

4 5- to 7-ounce tilapia fillets, rinsed and patted dry

2 cups store-bought or homemade tomato salsa

1 15-ounce can black beans, drained and rinsed

2 cups fresh pineapple, diced

2 limes, thinly sliced into rounds

1. Preheat the oven to 400°F.

2. Combine the rice and chicken broth in a pot over medium heat and bring to a boil. Cook until the liquid is below the surface of the rice and tunnels form in the rice. Reduce the heat to low and cover. Cook until the rice is tender, about 20 minutes.

3. Whisk together the orange juice, lime juice, oil, 2 tablespoons of cilantro, garlic, and sugar in a non-reactive medium bowl. Season with salt and pepper. Add the tilapia fillets to the marinade, turning to coat. Cover and refrigerate for 20 minutes, turning the tilapia occasionally in the marinade.

4. Stir together the cooked rice, salsa, beans, pineapple, and remaining 2 tablespoons of the cilantro in a 2- to 3-quart shallow baking dish. Remove the tilapia from the marinade, reserving the marinade, and arrange the fish over the rice mixture, overlapping if necessary. Pour the reserved marinade over the fish. Arrange the lime slices on top. Bake until the fish is opaque when flaked in the thickest part with the tip of a knife, 25 to 30 minutes. Sprinkle with chopped cilantro and serve hot.

latin-asian tuna ceviche

I love combining Latin and Asian flavors because they complement each other in unique ways. For example, the mirin enhances the flavor of the crunchy jicama. The tuna can be replaced with shrimp, crabmeat, or fish fillets. For a knockout presentation at parties, I put individual servings of ceviche on teaspoons on a tray.

MAKES 4 SERVINGS

1 8-ounce sushi-grade tuna steak, cut into ½-inch dice

¼ cup fresh orange juice

2 tablespoons fresh lemon juice

2 tablespoons fresh lime juice

2 tablespoons soy sauce

2 tablespoons mirin

1 teaspoon hot chili oil

1 teaspoon freshly grated ginger

¼ teaspoon kosher salt

½ small jicama, peeled and cut into ½-inch dice (about 2 cups)

1 8¼-ounce can mandarin oranges, drained and rinsed

1 cup cherry tomatoes, halved

¼ cup red onion, thinly sliced

1. Combine the tuna, orange juice, lemon juice, and lime juice in a large nonreactive bowl. Cover and refrigerate until the fish turns opaque, about 25 minutes; drain.

2. Whisk together the soy sauce, mirin, chili oil, ginger, and salt in a large bowl. Add the tuna, jicama, oranges, tomatoes, and onion. Cover and refrigerate until chilled, at least 1 hour, but no longer than 4 hours. Spoon the ceviche into small bowls or onto spoons and serve.

veracruz-style red snapper

There are endless versions of this Mexican dish from the seafood-rich waters of coastal Veracruz. While I like mine with a blend of the New World—Mexican tomatoes and chiles—and the Old World—capers and olive oil—I encourage you to adapt this preparation to your liking. The raisins are not part of the traditional recipe, but I like the added touch of a sprinkle of sweet in between the salt and tart flavor.

MAKES 4 SERVINGS

cooking spray

2 tablespoons olive oil

½ white onion, finely chopped

3 garlic cloves, minced

1 28-ounce can diced San Marzano tomatoes

⅓ cup green olives, pitted and chopped

3 tablespoons fresh parsley, finely chopped

2 tablespoons golden raisins

1 tablespoon fresh oregano, finely chopped

1 tablespoon capers

3 bay leaves

1 jalapeño pepper, unseeded and finely chopped

½ teaspoon salt

4 6-ounce red snapper fillets

1. Preheat the oven to 425°F. Spray a 9 × 13-inch baking dish with cooking spray.

2. Heat the oil in a large nonstick skillet over medium heat. Add the onion and garlic and cook, stirring occasionally, until the onion is tender, about 8 minutes. Add the tomatoes, olives, parsley, raisins, oregano, capers, bay leaves, jalapeño, and salt; bring to a boil. Reduce the heat and simmer, stirring frequently, until the flavors are blended and the sauce begins to bubble and thicken slightly, about 10 minutes.

3. Spread half of the sauce evenly on the bottom of the baking dish. Place the fillets on top of the sauce. Spoon the remaining sauce evenly over the fillets. Bake, uncovered, until the sauce is bubbly and the fish is opaque in the center, 12 to 15 minutes.

CHICA TIP

! Make a double batch of the sauce and refrigerate or freeze it to use on steamed vegetables or with scrambled or poached eggs.

corn-chile-crusted tilapia with banana curry sauce

When my friend was dieting, she was, of course, bored with the food she was eating. I was determined to show her that healthful food doesn't mean bland food and came up with this flavor-packed preparation. She couldn't believe how good it tasted. This is one of my all-time favorite fish recipes. Whether you're watching your weight or not, make it one of yours, too.

MAKES 4 SERVINGS

sauce:

1½ teaspoons olive oil

2 tablespoons rice wine vinegar

2 small ripe bananas, cut into 1-inch chunks

½ cup sweet onion, such as Vidalia, finely chopped

3 tablespoons shallot, finely chopped

2 garlic cloves, finely chopped

1 tablespoon plus 1½ teaspoons curry powder

2 teaspoons ground coriander

1½ cups reduced-sodium chicken broth

tilapia:

cooking spray

½ cup yellow cornmeal

1 teaspoon sweet paprika

1 teaspoon chili powder

pinch of kosher salt

4 4- to 5-ounce tilapia fillets, rinsed and patted dry with paper towels

chopped fresh cilantro, for serving

freshly grated zest of 1 lemon, for serving

1. To make the sauce, heat the oil in a medium nonstick skillet over medium heat until shimmering but not smoking. Add the rice wine vin-egar, bananas, onion, shallot, garlic, curry powder, and coriander and cook, stirring occasionally, until the mixture is fragrant, about 1 minute. Add the broth and bring to a boil. Reduce the heat to low and simmer until the onion is tender, about 5 minutes. Cool slightly. In batches, puree in a blender with the lid ajar. Return to the skillet and keep warm over very low heat.

2. Position the broiler rack 4 inches from the source of heat and preheat the broiler.

3. Line the broiler pan with aluminum foil and spray with cooking spray. Mix the cornmeal, paprika, chili powder, and salt together on a plate. Coat the fish evenly with the cornmeal mixture, shake off the excess, and arrange on the broiler pan. Spray the fillets with oil.

4. Broil until the tops of the fish are golden brown, about 4 minutes. Carefully turn the fillets and broil until the other side is browned, about 4 minutes more.

5. Place one fillet on each plate. Top with curry sauce and garnish with chopped cilantro and a bit of lemon zest. Serve immediately.

easy-breezy yellowtail packet

Yellowtail is a luscious fish with light red flesh and tender texture. Considered by many to be the most flavorful among the snapper family, the fish has a mild sweetness that can easily be overpowered by too much seasoning. To maintain its natural delicious flavor, I dress yellowtail with nothing more than parsley, oregano, and lemon.

MAKES 2 SERVINGS

¼ cup fresh flat-leaf parsley, plus more for garnish, chopped

freshly grated zest of 1 lemon

1 tablespoon fresh lemon juice

1 tablespoon fresh oregano leaves, finely chopped

1 jalapeño, seeded and minced

1 teaspoon capers

1 teaspoon Worcestershire sauce

1 garlic clove, minced

1 small zucchini, cut in ½-inch rounds

1 small yellow squash, cut in ½-inch rounds

2 6-ounce yellowtail or grouper fillets

½ teaspoon kosher salt

1 lemon, cut into 6 rounds

2 teaspoons olive oil

1. Preheat the oven to 400°F.

2. Stir the parsley, lemon zest, lemon juice, oregano, jalapeño, capers, Worcestershire sauce, and garlic in a medium bowl until combined.

3. Cut two 16 × 13-inch pieces of parchment paper. Fold each in half vertically to make 8 × 13-inch sides. Cut each into a wide half-heart shape, with the crease as the center of the heart. Unfold.

4. For each serving, place half of the zucchini and yellow squash on a parchment heart near the crease, sprinkle with a quarter of the parsley mixture, and top with a yellowtail fillet. Season with salt. Top with another quarter of the parsley mixture and 3 lemon slices. Drizzle with 1 teaspoon of oil. Brush the outer edges of parchment with olive oil, then fold. Fold the parchment over to re-create the half-heart and tightly crimp the open sides together, folding firmly every inch or so to tightly seal the parcel. Transfer the parchment hearts to a large baking sheet.

5. Bake until the parchment packets are puffed and you can hear the juices in the packets sizzling, about 15 minutes.

6. With a wide spatula, transfer each packet to a plate. Carefully open the packets, sprinkle the contents with parsley, and serve at once.

orange-basil salmon packets

Cooking fish, chicken, and vegetables in parchment paper is a technique that's too often overlooked by home cooks. All you have to do is layer the ingredients on a piece of the paper, seal it tightly, and pop it in the oven. Once the packet is cooked, transfer it to a plate and slice open the paper. The aromas and fresh flavors will immediately rise up. Best of all, there's little cleanup. Just toss the parchment paper when you're done. Once you try this method, you can adapt it with shrimp, scallops, and chicken cutlets. If you don't have any parchment paper on hand, use aluminum foil.

MAKES 2 SERVINGS

1 small fennel bulb with fronds, core removed, sliced thin, fronds reserved

2 6-ounce skinless salmon fillets

kosher salt

freshly ground black pepper

2 carrots, peeled and cut on the diagonal into ½-inch pieces

½ pound large asparagus, sliced on the diagonal into 1-inch pieces

½ cup fresh orange juice

zest of 1 orange

6 tablespoons plus 2 tablespoons fresh basil leaves, chopped

1 garlic clove, minced

2 tablespoons fresh fennel fronds (the dill-like greens on the fennel bulb), chopped

2 teaspoons olive oil

1. Preheat the oven to 400°F.

2. Cut two 16 × 13 inch pieces of parchment paper. Fold each in half vertically, so you have 8 × 13-inch sides. Cut each into a wide half-heart shape, with the crease as the center of the heart. Unfold.

3. For each serving, place half of the fennel slices on a parchment heart near the crease. Top with a salmon fillet and season with salt and pepper. Surround the salmon with half of the carrots and asparagus. Stir together the orange juice and zest, 6 tablespoons of the basil, and garlic, and season with salt and pepper. Pour half of mixture evenly over the salmon. Top with half of the chopped fennel fronds. Brush the outer edges of parchment with olive oil; then fold the parchment over to re-create the half-heart, and tightly crimp the open sides together, folding firmly every inch or so to tightly seal the parcel.

4. Bake until the packets are puffed and you can hear the juices inside the packet sizzling, 10 to 13 minutes. Using a wide spatula, transfer each packet to a dinner plate. Carefully open the packets, sprinkle the contents with the remaining basil and fennel fronds, and serve immediately.

CHICA TIP

! ■ Try this technique with grouper, cod, flounder, or halibut. Instead of the carrots and asparagus mentioned above, try sugar snaps, thinly sliced zucchini or yellow squash, sliced mushrooms, or cherry tomatoes.

mirin and garlic pan-steamed salmon

Here's a Latin-Asian spin on a simple fish preparation. Mirin is a low-alcohol, pale-in-color wine made from rice. Look for it in Asian or general supermarkets.

MAKES 4 SERVINGS

4 6-ounce skinless salmon fillets

kosher salt

freshly ground black pepper

1 tablespoon olive oil

1 medium yellow onion, thinly sliced

4 garlic cloves, minced

2 tablespoons mirin

2 tablespoons water

2 cups fresh cilantro, coarsely chopped

lime wedges, for serving

CHICA TIP

! **When buying salmon, pay close attention to the signs that are placed in the ice with the fish. Farm-raised salmon is often artificially colored, and it will say so on the sign. If not, ask. And don't buy it.**

1. Season both sides of the salmon fillets with salt and pepper and set aside.

2. Heat the olive oil in a very large skillet over medium-high heat. Add the onion and garlic and cook until the onions are soft and starting to brown, 6 to 8 minutes, stirring often. Add 1 table-spoon of mirin and stir, scraping up the browned bits in the pan with a wooden spoon, and cook until the mirin has evaporated, about 30 seconds. Reduce the heat to medium. Place the salmon side by side in the skillet. Add the remaining mirin and enough water to barely cover the bottom of the skillet (about 2 tablespoons). Bring the liquid to a simmer, cover the skillet and re-duce the heat to low. Cook gently until the salmon is mostly opaque with a pink center when flaked in the thickest part with the tip of a knife, 8 to 10 minutes.

3. Sprinkle with the cilantro. Transfer each salmon fillet with ¼ of the pan sauce to a dinner plate. Serve hot, with the lime wedges.

smoky chipotle shrimp

Canned chipotle peppers are my secret ingredient when I want to add a boost of flavor to my cooking. Their smokiness, heat, and vinegary taste add flavor to just about any dish. I keep cans of chipotle in adobo sauce in my pantry. This simple shrimp preparation will be on the table almost as fast as you can say, "One, two, three."

cooking spray

2 large tomatoes, cut into quarters

1 medium onion, cut into quarters

2 garlic cloves

3 chipotle chiles in adobo plus 1 tablespoon adobo sauce

1 pound large shrimp, peeled and deveined, tails left on

½ teaspoon kosher salt

½ teaspoon freshly ground black pepper

2 tablespoons olive oil

⅓ cup dry white wine, such as pinot grigio

¼ cup fresh lime juice

1 teaspoon fresh oregano leaves, chopped

¼ cup fresh cilantro, chopped, for serving

1. To make the sauce, position the broiler rack about 5 inches from the heat source and preheat the broiler.

2. Spray the broiler pan with cooking spray. Place the tomato and onion quarters and garlic on the rack. Spray the vegetables with cooking spray. Broil, turning occasionally, until the vegetables are softened and charred around the edges, 8 to 10 minutes. Let cool for 10 minutes.

3. Transfer the tomatoes, onion, and garlic to a food processor. Add the chipotles and adobo sauce and puree.

4. Meanwhile, spray a large nonstick skillet with cooking spray and heat over medium-high heat. Season the shrimp with salt and pepper. Add to the skillet and cook, stirring occasionally, until just opaque in the center, about 3 to 5 minutes. Transfer the shrimp to a plate.

5. Add the olive oil to the skillet and heat over medium heat. Add the chipotle puree, wine, and lime juice and bring to a boil. Reduce the heat to medium low and simmer, stirring occasionally, until the sauce is lightly thickened, about 10 minutes. Return the shrimp to the skillet, add the oregano, and cook just until the shrimp is reheated, about 1 minute. Season to taste with salt and pepper. Remove from heat, stir in the cilantro, and serve hot.

lime shrimp boil

My Latin version of an old-fashioned New England shrimp boil takes this classic to a whole new *chica* level. I use lime, Colombian chorizo, cilantro, and jalapeño to give this an unexpected twist. In New England, the cooking liquid is usually discarded, but the broth in this dish is so delicious that I now serve it as well. My favorite presentation is to cover my table with banana or palm leaves, drain the shrimp, sausage, and vegetables and pile them on the table. Keep the warm broth in a large pot or other container and serve in bowls.

MAKES 6 SERVINGS

dipping sauce:

1 cup mayonnaise (regular or light)

½ cup Dijon mustard

2 teaspoons honey

1 teaspoon Worcestershire sauce

4 cups store-bought seafood stock

2 cups water

1 medium yellow onion, cut into quarters

1 bunch cilantro sprigs, tied with kitchen twine

¼ cup fresh lime juice

4 garlic cloves, crushed under a knife and peeled

1 jalapeño, seeded and quartered

2 teaspoons Delicioso Adobo Seasoning (page 8)

1 teaspoon kosher salt

1 bay leaf

1½ pounds red baby potatoes

¾ pound Andouille or pre-cooked Colombian sausage or other smoked sausage, cut into 2-inch lengths

2 ears fresh corn, husked and cut in thirds

1½ pounds jumbo shrimp, peeled and deveined

lime wedges, for serving

¼ cup fresh cilantro, chopped

hot red pepper sauce, for serving

1. To make the dipping sauce, combine the ingredients in a small bowl until blended. Cover with plastic wrap and refrigerate until ready to serve.

2. Bring the broth, water, onion, tied cilantro, lime juice, garlic, jalapeño, adobo seasoning, salt, and bay leaf to a boil in a large stockpot. Boil for 10 minutes.

3. Add the potatoes and cook until almost tender, about 15 minutes. Add the sausage and corn and cook until the potatoes are tender, about 10 minutes more. Remove from the heat and stir in the shrimp. Cover the pot and let stand 3 minutes, or until the shrimp turn pink. Discard the tied cilantro.

4. Using a slotted spoon or wire skimmer, transfer the potatoes, shrimp, sausage, and corn to a large platter and add the lime wedges. Sprinkle with the chopped cilantro. Ladle the broth into soup bowls. Spoon the dipping sauce into individual bowls. Serve the shrimp mixture hot, with the dipping sauce, with the dipping sauce and the hot sauce passed on the side.

catalan noodle paella (*fideuà*)

Fideuà, a regional specialty from Catalonia, uses thin pasta instead of rice in this paella. The noodles are first browned; then all the other ingredients and a saffron-laced broth are added. This recipe uses mussels and calamari but feel free to substitute shrimp, clams, and chorizo.

MAKES 6 TO 8 SERVINGS

2 tablespoons olive oil

12 ounces whole-wheat angel hair pasta, broken into quarters

1 large yellow onion, finely chopped

4 garlic cloves, minced

1 14.5-ounce can diced tomatoes in juice

1⅔ cups store-bought seafood broth

⅓ cup dry sherry or dry white wine, such as pinot grigio

1 teaspoon sweet paprika, preferably Spanish

½ teaspoon saffron threads, crushed

⅛ teaspoon ground cinnamon

2½ dozen mussels, scrubbed and debearded, if necessary

1 pound fresh or frozen thawed calamari, cleaned and cut into ½-inch rings

1 cup thawed frozen peas

2 tablespoons fresh flat-leaf parsley, chopped

½ teaspoon kosher salt

¼ teaspoon freshly ground black pepper

lemon wedges, for serving

1. Heat the oil in a large paella pan or skillet with a 12- to 14-inch diameter over medium heat. Add the pasta and cook, turning often with kitchen tongs, until it starts to brown, about 2 minutes.

2. Push the pasta to one side of the pan. Add the onion and garlic to the cleared side of the pan and cook, stirring occasionally, until tender, about 5 minutes. Combine the pasta with the vegetables. Stir in the tomatoes with their juices, broth, sherry, paprika, saffron, and cinnamon and bring to a simmer. Add the mussels, calamari, peas, and parsley. Reduce the heat to medium low and cover.

3. Simmer until the pasta is tender, the mussels begin to open, and the calamari is opaque, 8 to 10 minutes. Remove and discard any mussels that do not open. Season with salt and pepper. Serve hot from the pan with the lemon wedges.

shrimp and scallop easy paella

When making paella, "easy" isn't the first word you may think of. My recipe will change your mind. This easy version will make you look like a professional chef.

6 cups low-sodium chicken broth

3 tablespoons extra-virgin olive oil

1 medium onion, chopped

4 garlic cloves, minced

1 red bell pepper, seeded, ribbed, and thinly sliced

1 green bell pepper, seeded, ribbed, and thinly sliced

1 teaspoon Spanish saffron threads

4 links Spanish dry-cured chorizo (about 6 ounces), sliced

1½ cups white rice

1 10-ounce can diced tomatoes with chiles

3 tablespoons tomato paste

kosher salt

freshly ground black pepper

2 pounds raw, peeled large shrimp

1 pound sea scallops, patted dry

⅓ cup flat-leaf parsley leaves, chopped, for serving

lemon wedges, for serving

1. In a medium saucepan, heat the chicken broth until boiling.

2. In a separate large skillet or paella pan over medium-high heat, heat the oil. When the oil is hot, add the onion, garlic, peppers, saffron, and chorizo. Cook for 6 minutes or until the vegetables are soft and the chorizo is browned.

3. Stir in the rice, diced tomatoes, and tomato paste until well mixed and cook for 5 minutes. Add the boiling chicken broth, little by little, stirring each addition constantly until the broth is almost absorbed. Salt and pepper to taste.

4. Cover the pan with aluminum foil, reduce the heat to medium low, and cook for 20 to 25 minutes, until the rice is tender.

5. Season the shrimp and scallops with salt and pepper. Remove the aluminum foil from the pan and add the seafood. Cover with the aluminum foil and let simmer for 5 to 7 minutes, until the seafood is cooked through.

6. Garnish with chopped parsley and lemon wedges before serving.

pan-seared trout with peruvian creole sauce

In Peru, this dish is called *Trucha a la Criolla*. *Criolla* is a sauce most often served with fish. It's made of tomato and onions that are slightly pickled in an *ají amarillo*–lime vinaigrette. Soaking the raw onions in water for ten minutes eliminates some of the strong taste but leaves just enough of their flavor.

MAKES 4 SERVINGS

1 large red onion, cut into thin half-moons

1½ teaspoons kosher salt

1 small tomato, chopped

¼ cup fresh lime juice

¼ cup fresh cilantro, chopped

2 tablespoons distilled white vinegar

¾ teaspoon *ají amarillo* paste

1 teaspoon olive oil

1 tablespoon unsalted butter

4 6-ounce trout fillets with skin

½ teaspoon freshly ground black pepper

1. Place the onion in a large bowl and sprinkle with 1 teaspoon of salt. Add enough water to cover. Let stand 10 minutes. Drain, rinse under cold running water, drain again, and pat dry.

2. Return the onion to the bowl. Add the tomato, lime juice, cilantro, vinegar, and *ají amarillo* paste. Let stand for 15 minutes.

3. Heat the oil and butter in a large nonstick skillet over medium-high heat. Sprinkle the trout with the remaining ½ teaspoon salt and the pepper. Add the trout to the skillet, skin side down, and cook until the skin is crispy, about 5 minutes. Turn and cook just until the trout flesh is lightly browned and opaque when flaked in the center with the tip of a knife (turn the trout to check), about 2 minutes.

4. Transfer the trout, skin side down, to a platter. Spoon the onion mixture on top and serve immediately.

coconut-almond-crusted codfish

Here's a minimalist preparation that speaks to my belief that when it comes to fish, less is more. Fish fillets are often dipped in egg, then dredged with flour, dipped again in the egg, and then dipped into bread crumbs and fried in oil. For a lighter Latin version, I dip cod fillets in coconut milk, then dredge the pieces in a blend of coconut flakes and almond meal, and bake them until crisp.

MAKES 4 SERVINGS

cooking spray

¾ cup sliced almonds

½ cup sweetened coconut flakes

¼ cup unsweetened coconut milk (not cream of coconut)

1 teaspoon fresh lime juice

4 6-ounce cod fillets

½ teaspoon kosher salt

lime wedges, for serving

1. Preheat the oven to 425°F.

2. Spray a baking pan with cooking spray. Pulse the almonds and coconut in a food processor until coarsely ground, about 10 seconds. Place the almond mixture on a sheet of wax paper. Whisk together the coconut milk and lime juice in a pie plate until blended.

3. Sprinkle the fillets with the salt. Dip the fillets, one piece at a time, into the coconut milk mixture, then into the almond mixture, pressing to adhere. Place the fillets in the baking pan. Lightly spray with cooking spray.

4. Bake, without turning, until the topping is browned and the fish is opaque when pierced in the center with the tip of a knife, about 10 minutes. Serve immediately with lime wedges.

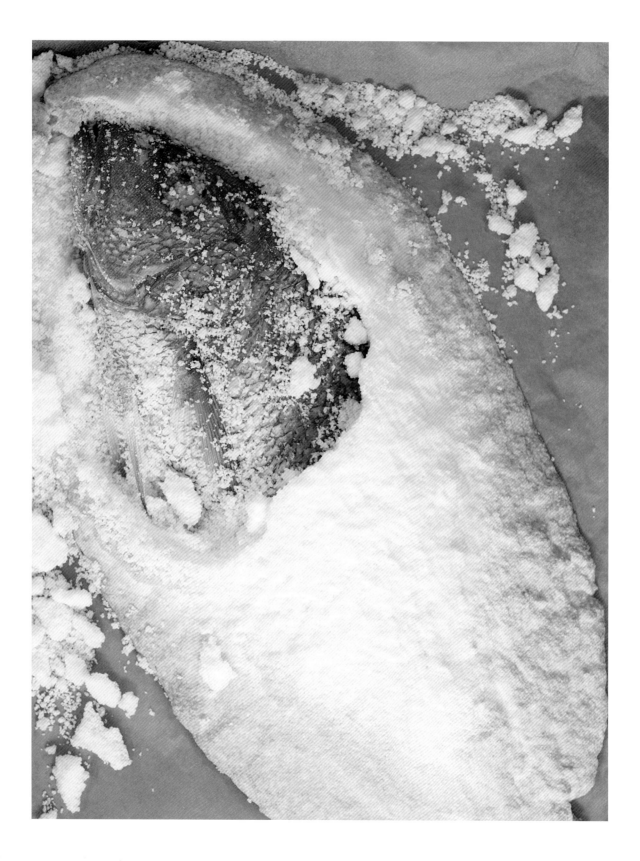

whole fish baked in salt

Your guests will be amazed when you bring a fish encased in a salt crust to the table. When you crack the crust, the most amazing aroma will waft through the air. And no, the fish won't be salty at all, just moist, with a hint of the sea.

MAKES 4 SERVINGS

1 48-ounce box kosher salt

3 large egg whites

⅓ cup water

1 lemon, halved crosswise

6 fresh flat-leaf parsley sprigs

1 2-pound whole red snapper, cleaned, head and tail intact

extra-virgin olive oil, for drizzling

2 tablespoons fresh flat-leaf parsley, chopped, for serving

1. Preheat the oven to 450°F. Line a large baking sheet with parchment paper or foil.

2. Combine the salt, egg whites, and water in a large bowl, stirring until a thick paste forms. Place half of the salt mixture onto the baking sheet, spreading it in a rectangle just slightly larger than the fish.

3. Cut 1 lemon half into 4 rounds. Stuff the lemon slices and parsley sprigs into the cavity of the fish, then place the fish on top of the salt paste. Mound the remaining salt paste onto the fish, pressing and shaping the paste to cover the fish completely. Roast until the salt crust looks dry and set, about 30 minutes. Remove from the oven.

4. Crack the crust with the back of a large spoon; then carefully remove the crust in chunks. With a sharp knife and a wide fork, lift the top fillets from the snapper and transfer to dinner plates. Lift off and discard the fish's bones, and transfer the remaining fillets to plates. Squeeze the lemon juice from the remaining lemon half over the fillets, drizzle with olive oil, and sprinkle with the chopped parsley. Serve immediately.

CHICA TIP

! If your fish weighs more than 2½ pounds, add 5 minutes' cooking time for each additional pound.

chicalicious lobster sandwich

I was so pleased when I learned that my Chicalicious Lobster Roll was a contender in Oprah's Sandwich Showdown. This ultradecadent sandwich is no wimpy lobster roll. It's overflowing with succulent poached lobster that's lightly coated with chipotle mayonnaise, avocado, and fresh herbs. Crowning it all is a creamy poached egg and crisp bacon. It might be messy, but who cares? It's that good!

MAKES 4 SERVINGS

chipotle mayonnaise:

¾ cup mayonnaise

3 chipotle chiles in adobo, seeded and chopped

2 garlic cloves, chopped

1 shallot, chopped

1 tablespoon fresh lemon juice

lobster:

5 fresh basil leaves

3 3-inch sprigs fresh tarragon

1 teaspoon pure vanilla extract

½ teaspoon black peppercorns

4 frozen lobster tails in the shell, thawed

8 slices thick-cut bacon

4 large eggs

1 teaspoon white distilled or cider vinegar

kosher salt

2 tablespoons unsalted butter

4 challah or brioche buns, toasted

1 ripe Hass avocado, halved, peeled, pitted, and sliced

freshly ground black pepper

fresh chives, chopped, for garnish

1. To make the chipotle mayonnaise, pulse the mayonnaise, chipotles, garlic, shallot, and lemon juice in a food processor until well combined.

2. To steam the lobster, pour about 2 quarts of water into a large pot with a steamer insert, being sure the water doesn't touch the bottom of the insert. Add the basil, tarragon, vanilla, and peppercorns to the water and bring to a boil over medium heat. Add the lobster and cover tightly. Steam for 8 to 12 minutes until the lobster shells are bright red. (The lobster should be slightly undercooked and translucent since it will be further cooked in butter.) Remove the steamed lobster tails from the pot and place on a cutting board. Let cool until easy to handle. Remove the lobster meat, discarding the shells. Cut the lobster meat crosswise into ½-inch-thick pieces.

3. Meanwhile, cook the bacon in a large skillet over medium heat, turning occasionally, until crisp and browned, about 8 minutes. Using tongs, place cooked bacon on a few sheets of paper towels to drain, leaving the fat in the pan. Set the skillet aside.

4. While the bacon is cooking, poach the eggs. Fill a deep skillet with water, add the vinegar and a pinch of salt, and bring to a simmer over medium-low heat. Reduce the heat so the water is just below a simmer. One at a time, crack each egg into a small bowl, and slide the egg into the simmering water. Cook until the whites are set and the centers are still soft, about 3 minutes.

5. Using a slotted spoon, transfer the poached eggs to a paper towel–lined plate.

6. Add the butter to the fat in the skillet. Stir over medium heat until the butter is melted. Add the lobster meat, turning to coat in the fat, and cook until slightly golden, about 3 minutes. For each sandwich, spread about 2 tablespoons of the mayonnaise on a toasted bun. Layer a few slices of avocado over the bottom of the bun, and top with ¼ of the lobster and 2 bacon slices. Add a poached egg, season with salt and pepper, and sprinkle with chives. Return the bun top to the sandwich and serve immediately.

rosemary butter beans

on the side

My issue with side dishes is that they're usually either too heavy, too boring, or too fattening. Yes, a side dish should never take away from the main dish, but rather complement it. But this doesn't mean it should be boring or lack flavor! When people think of healthful side dishes, they often think of a side salad or steamed vegetables. That's just too plain and boring for me. I love my side dishes with a little kick, such as Anchovy-Spiked Broccoli or Parsley-and-Chile-Crusted Baked Plantains.

The right side dishes are key to balancing out a meal and incorporating much-needed nutrients into our diet. Eat earthy proteins like beans and quinoa and healthful complex carbohydrates like brown rice and tubers (sweet potatoes and malanga). These are the basics in Latin cooking, and nothing beats a bowl of rice and beans! They don't have to be fattening. It's all about how you prepare them and portion control.

Many recipes in this chapter can be doubled and frozen for future use. (Beans and tubers tend to freeze well, as long as they are properly sealed and packed. Label and date the containers.)

These sides are the ones that will turn the fish or chicken you just brought home from the market into a complete and satisfying meal.

nicaraguan red beans and rice
(gallo pinto)

This is my light version of *gallo pinto*, or "spotted rooster," a humble rendition of red beans and rice served throughout Central America. Though the type of the bean varies from country to country, region to region, the dish is traditionally made with leftover rice. When eaten together, beans and rice provide all the essential amino acids—the building blocks of protein and muscles in the body—that we need.

MAKES 4 SERVINGS

2 tablespoons olive oil

2 large yellow onions, thinly sliced

2 garlic cloves, minced

2 cups cooked white rice

1 15½-ounce can red kidney beans, drained and rinsed

¼ cup low-sodium chicken broth

1 teaspoon ground cumin

salt, to taste

pepper, to taste

¼ cup fresh cilantro, chopped

Heat the oil in a large saucepan over medium-high heat. Add the onions and garlic and cook, stirring occasionally, until the onions are golden and tender, about 5 minutes. Stir in the rice, beans, broth, cumin, salt, and pepper and bring to a boil. Reduce the heat to medium low and simmer, stirring occasionally, until the flavors are blended, 5 to 7 minutes. Remove from the heat. Stir in the cilantro and serve hot.

on the side

caramelized onions and lentil rice

Much of Latin cuisine has its origins in the Middle East, first brought to Spain by the Moors, then on to other parts of the Spanish empire. Mujaddara, made with lentils and rice and topped with caramelized onion, is such a dish. This dish makes a great replacement for animal protein.

MAKES 4 TO 6 SERVINGS

1 tablespoon unsalted butter

2 tablespoons olive oil

1 medium onion, thinly sliced

1 teaspoon sugar

kosher salt

freshly ground black pepper

2 garlic cloves, minced

¾ cup dried lentils

4¼ cups water

¼ teaspoon ground cumin

1½ cups long-grain white rice

1. Melt the butter with 1 tablespoon oil in a medium skillet over low heat. Add the onion, sugar, and some salt and pepper. Cook until the onions become deep brown and sticky, about 20 to 25 minutes, stirring every 4 or 5 minutes.

2. Heat the remaining tablespoon of oil in a saucepan over medium heat. Add the garlic and cook, stirring, until fragrant, 30 seconds to 1 minute. Add the lentils, water, and cumin. Increase heat to medium high and bring to a boil. Reduce the heat to low, cover, and cook 15 minutes. Uncover and turn the heat to medium high. Add the rice and bring to a boil. Reduce the heat to low; cover and cook until the rice is tender and has absorbed all of the liquid, about 20 minutes. Serve topped with the caramelized onions.

on the side

rosemary butter beans

Butter beans are a good source of dietary fiber and a virtually fat-free source of high-quality protein. This quick and healthful dish is spruced up with piney rosemary, garlic, and champagne vinegar, making it a great side that goes well with pork chops.

MAKES 4 TO 6 SERVINGS

1 head garlic

½ large sweet onion, such as Vidalia, cut into 2-inch chunks

2 3-inch sprigs fresh rosemary

olive oil

kosher salt

freshly ground black pepper

2 15-ounce cans butter beans

1 tablespoon champagne vinegar

1. Preheat the oven to 375°F.

2. Cut off the top fourth of the garlic head and peel off the loose skin. Place the head, cut side up, on a 12-inch square of aluminum foil. Add the onion, a sprig of rosemary, and a drizzle of olive oil. Season with salt and pepper to taste. Wrap the garlic in the foil and place on a baking sheet. Bake until the garlic is very tender, about 50 minutes. Let cool until easy to handle.

3. Meanwhile, drain 1 can of beans in a wire sieve and rinse under cold running water. Transfer to a medium saucepan and add the remaining beans with their liquid. Chop the leaves from the remaining rosemary and add to the beans. Bring to a simmer over medium heat, reduce the heat to medium low and simmer until the beans are hot, about 7 minutes.

4. Squeeze half of the roasted garlic cloves, roasted onion, and vinegar onto the beans and stir. Season with salt and pepper. Serve hot.

salt-and-vinegar chipotle-roasted potatoes

I love salt-and-vinegar potato chips, but my waistline doesn't. I bake, rather than fry, russet potato wedges tossed with kosher salt, chipotle powder, vinegar, and some olive oil for those same flavors, but with fewer calories. This satisfies my craving!

MAKES 4 TO 6 SERVINGS

¼ cup red wine vinegar

½ teaspoon ground cumin

1 teaspoon chipotle powder

6 small or 4 large russet potatoes

¼ cup olive oil

2 tablespoons kosher salt

1 tablespoon coarse black pepper

1 small red onion, cut lengthwise into sixths

1. Preheat the oven to 350°F.

2. In a large bowl, mix vinegar, cumin, and chipotle powder.

3. Cut potatoes into 1-inch chunks. Add the potatoes to the vinegar mixture and toss well. Let marinate for 5 to 10 minutes.

4. Drizzle the oil over the potatoes and toss. Spread in a single layer in a large rimmed baking pan or roasting dish. Season with the salt and pepper. Roast uncovered for 40 minutes, stirring occasionally.

5. Remove the baking sheet with the potatoes from the oven. Add the onion wedges and toss to coat with the pan juices. Return the baking sheet to the oven and roast until the potatoes are browned and tender, about 20 minutes more.

CHICA TIP

If you are watching your carbs, parsnips are a great substitute for potatoes. They work especially well for roasted potato recipes. You can start by substituting just half of the potatoes.

on the side

spaghetti squash hash browns

This oblong winter squash is super low in calories, packed with good-for-you beta-carotene found in yellow and orange vegetables, and can be cooked in many ways—baked, steamed, microwaved, or boiled. Best of all, the cooked squash looks—and can be treated—like thin spaghetti when raked with a fork.

MAKES 4 SERVINGS

olive oil cooking spray

1 2-pound spaghetti squash, halved lengthwise

cooking spray

1 tablespoon olive oil

1 medium yellow onion, thinly sliced

½ teaspoon kosher salt

¼ teaspoon chili powder

¼ teaspoon achiote powder

¼ teaspoon freshly ground black pepper

1. Preheat the oven to 400°F. Line a baking pan just large enough to hold the squash halves with parchment paper or aluminum foil and lightly spray with olive oil cooking spray.

2. Lightly spray the squash halves with olive oil and place, cut side down, in the baking pan. Bake until the squash is tender when pierced with the tip of a sharp knife, about 45 minutes.

3. Flip the squash over and let cool 5 minutes. Scoop out and discard the seeds. With the tines of a fork, scrape the squash into a large bowl and discard the skin.

4. Meanwhile, heat the olive oil in a large non-stick skillet over medium-high heat. Add the onion, salt, chili powder, achiote powder, and pepper. Cook, stirring occasionally, until the onion is tender, about 5 minutes.

5. Add the squash and mix gently. Cook, undisturbed, until the underside of the squash begins to brown, about 3 minutes. Cook, tossing occasionally, until lightly browned, 6 to 8 minutes. Serve hot.

CHICA TIP

Add cooked spaghetti squash to soups in place of noodles. Toss it with olive oil, chopped parsley, and shaved Parmesan or *queso blanco* or mix it with chopped tomatoes, capers, basil or oregano, and olive oil for a gluten-free "pasta."

stewed pigeon peas

Throughout Latin America and the Caribbean, rice and beans are eaten every day, sometimes three times a day. In Puerto Rico, *arroz con gandules* (rice with pigeon peas) is the local favorite. Although they're beans, pigeon peas range in color from creamy white to pea green and look a bit like peas. I cook the pigeon peas with butternut squash and tomatoes for a colorful vegetable side dish.

MAKES 4 TO 6 SERVINGS

2 cups frozen pigeon peas (*gandules*)

1 cup butternut squash, peeled and cubed (½ inch)

2 tablespoons olive oil

1 medium green bell pepper, cored and diced

1 medium yellow onion, chopped

3 garlic cloves, chopped

1 Roma (plum) tomato, diced

½ cup fresh cilantro, chopped

¼ cup *ají dulce* or *cachucha* peppers, seeded and chopped

½ teaspoon Delicioso Adobo Seasoning (page 8)

¾ cup reduced-sodium chicken broth

kosher salt, to taste

freshly ground black pepper

1. Bring a large saucepan of lightly salted water to a boil over high heat. Add the pigeon peas and squash and cook until the squash is al dente, about 15 minutes. Scoop out and reserve ½ cup of the cooking liquid; then drain the vegetables.

2. Heat the oil in a medium skillet over medium heat. Add the bell pepper and onion and cook until softened, about 2 minutes. Stir in the garlic, followed by the tomato, cilantro, *ají dulce*, and adobo seasoning. Cook until the tomato gives off some juices, about 3 minutes.

3. Add the pigeon peas and squash and stir well. Stir in the broth and reserved cooking liquid and bring to a simmer. Reduce the heat to low and simmer until the squash is tender, 8 to 10 minutes. Season with salt and pepper. Serve hot.

on the side

yellow pepper quinoa

Healthful, gluten-free quinoa has become one of my favorite ingredients. Protein-packed and high in fiber, calcium, and other nutrients, it is the superfood of all superfoods. I use quick-to-cook quinoa in salads, in soups, and in place of pasta. Use this preparation as a base for adding other ingredients—chopped vegetables, nuts, and leftover bits of chicken or meat. Once you try it, quinoa will become a staple in your kitchen.

MAKES 4 TO 6 SERVINGS

1½ cups quinoa

2½ cups water

2 tablespoons olive oil

2 tablespoons unsalted butter

1 medium yellow onion, chopped

1 medium green bell pepper, cored, seeded, ribbed, and chopped

2 garlic cloves, finely chopped

3 tablespoons fresh flat-leaf parsley leaves, plus more for serving, coarsely chopped

2 tablespoons Delicioso Adobo Seasoning (page 8)

¾ teaspoon Peruvian *aji amarillo* paste

kosher salt

1. Rinse the quinoa in a fine-mesh wire sieve under cold water. Drain and transfer to a medium saucepan. Add the water and bring to a boil over high heat. Reduce the heat to medium low and simmer until all of the grains have burst, about 20 minutes. Drain the cooked quinoa in the sieve.

2. Meanwhile, heat the oil and butter together in a large skillet over medium heat. Add the onion, green pepper, and garlic and cook, stirring occasionally, until the onion is translucent, about 5 minutes. Stir in 3 tablespoons of parsley, adobo, *aji amarillo*, and salt. Add the quinoa and mix well. Serve hot sprinkled with the remaining chopped parsley.

parsley-and-chili-crusted baked plantains

Plantains are a staple food in many parts of the world. Ripe plantains are usually fried and are the go-to side dish throughout the Caribbean. Plantains require steaming, frying, boiling, grilling, or, as in this dish, baking. Starchy plantains are another good-for-you side dish that's easy to make.

MAKES 4 TO 6 SERVINGS

cooking spray

4 ripe plantains

2 cups fresh flat-leaf parsley leaves, chopped

2 tablespoons chili powder

2 tablespoons olive oil

¾ teaspoon kosher salt

½ teaspoon freshly ground black pepper

1. Preheat the oven to 350°F. Spray a baking dish with cooking spray.

2. Using a small sharp knife, cut off the stem and tip from each plantain. Cut 4 slits down the entire length of each plantain, cutting just through the ridges on the peel to the flesh. With the tip of the knife, lift and remove the peel from the flesh.

3. Combine the parsley, chili powder, olive oil, salt, and pepper in a wide, shallow bowl. Roll each plantain in the parsley mixture to evenly coat. Transfer to the baking dish. Cut a piece of parchment paper to fit inside the baking dish. Cover the plantains with the parchment paper, and then tightly cover the dish with aluminum foil.

4. Bake until the plantains are tender when pierced with the tip of a sharp knife, about 40 minutes. Serve hot.

rice cooked in beer (*arroz en cerveza*)

I grew up eating rice every day. It's been hard to leave that tradition behind as I've learned more about nutrition. If I'm going to eat rice, then it had better be special! Beer gives rice a sweet and slightly nutty taste. Let your family and friends guess the secret ingredient.

MAKES 4 SERVINGS

½ teaspoon olive oil

¼ cup yellow onion, finely chopped

¼ cup carrot, finely diced

¼ cup water

1 cup white long-grain rice

1 12-ounce bottle lager, pilsner, or pale ale

1½ cups reduced-sodium chicken broth

¼ teaspoon ground turmeric

2 garlic cloves, crushed under a knife and peeled

½ teaspoon kosher salt

¼ teaspoon freshly ground black pepper

1. Heat the oil in a medium saucepan over medium heat. Add the onion, carrot, and water and cook, stirring often, until the water has evaporated and the vegetables soften, about 5 minutes. Add the rice and stir well. Stir in the beer, broth, turmeric, garlic, salt, and pepper. Bring to a boil over high heat. Reduce the heat to low and cover tightly. Simmer until the rice is tender and absorbs the liquid, 15 to 20 minutes. Remove from the heat.

2. Fluff the rice with a fork, discarding the garlic, and serve hot.

simple brown rice 101

It's back to basics with brown rice! Nutritionally, brown rice is better than its white counterpart—it's higher in fiber, vitamins, and minerals with a chewier texture and a nuttier flavor. The trade-off, however, is that cooking brown rice, or at least cooking it well, is tricky. I find that cooking brown rice in my pressure cooker guarantees perfect, moist rice every time. Once you try this method, you'll never cook brown rice any other way.

MAKES 4 SERVINGS

1¾ cups reduced-sodium chicken broth

1 cup short-grain brown rice

2 garlic cloves, crushed under a knife and peeled

2 teaspoons olive oil

½ teaspoon kosher salt

1. Stir the broth, brown rice, garlic, oil, and salt together in a pressure cooker. Cover with the cooker lid and, following the manufacturer's directions, bring the pressure up to high over high heat. Reduce the heat to low and continue cooking, maintaining a high pressure for 22 minutes. Remove from the heat. Let the pressure come down, and then let stand 10 minutes more.

2. Uncover the cooker. Fluff rice with a fork, discard the garlic, and serve hot.

malanga and roasted garlic mash

Malanga, similar to taro root, is a dark brown root with a creamy, speckled interior. I love it mashed with garlic, peppercorns, and buttermilk, like a potato.

1 teaspoon black peppercorns

2½ pounds white malanga, peeled and cut into 1-inch pieces

1 cup low-fat buttermilk

3 or 4 roasted garlic cloves (see *Chica Tip,* page 56)

½ teaspoon kosher salt

¼ teaspoon freshly ground black pepper

1. Tie the peppercorns in a double-thick packet of cheesecloth. Put the malanga and peppercorn packet into a large saucepan, and add enough cold water to cover. Bring to a boil over high heat. Reduce the heat to medium-low and cover. Simmer until the malanga is tender, about 30 minutes. Drain, discarding the peppercorn packet.

2. Return the malanga to the pot. Add the buttermilk and 3 or 4 roasted garlic cloves. Using a potato masher, coarsely mash the mixture, seasoning with salt and pepper. Serve hot.

on the side

pisto manchego

Pisto, a stew of eggplant, onion, zucchini, and peppers, comes from the area around La Mancha, Spain. Similar to ratatouille, it can be served as a *tapa* (appetizer) with a glass of sherry or wine or as a side dish with roasted and grilled meats. I put poached or fried eggs on top for a weekend brunch or weekday dinner. Sometimes I add some toasted pine nuts, raisins, or grated Manchego. Pisto is so versatile; offer it hot, cold, or at room temperature. Double or triple the recipe and freeze it.

MAKES 4 TO 6 SERVINGS

2 tablespoons olive oil

1 large yellow onion, diced

1 medium eggplant, cut into 1-inch pieces

2 large zucchini, cut into 1-inch pieces

2 large Roma (plum) tomatoes, cut into ½-inch dice

1 medium green bell pepper, cored, seeded, and ribbed, cut into ½-inch dice

1 medium red bell pepper, cored, seeded, and ribbed, cut into ½-inch dice

3 garlic cloves, minced

½ teaspoon kosher salt

¼ teaspoon freshly ground black pepper

2 teaspoons red wine vinegar

1 tablespoon fresh basil leaves, chopped, for serving

1. Heat the oil in a Dutch oven over medium-high heat. Add the onion and cook until tender, about 5 minutes. Add the eggplant, zucchini, tomatoes, bell peppers, garlic, salt, and pepper and bring to a boil. Reduce the heat to medium and cover.

2. Simmer, stirring occasionally, until the vegetables are tender, about 20 minutes. Remove from the heat and stir in the vinegar. Cool slightly. Sprinkle with the basil and serve warm or room temperature.

on the side

mojito sweeties mash

Orange-fleshed sweet potatoes have a custardy, dense, and creamy consistency. Adding lime and mint, the bright flavors of a mojito, gives the dish a Cuban spin.

MAKES 4 SERVINGS

2 large sweet potatoes, unpeeled (about 1½ pounds)

1 tablespoon olive oil

2 tablespoons fresh mint leaves, coarsely chopped

2 tablespoons fresh lime juice

½ teaspoon kosher salt

¼ teaspoon freshly ground black pepper

fresh mint sprigs, for garnish

1. Put the whole sweet potatoes in a large saucepan and add enough cold water to cover. Bring to a boil over high heat. Reduce the heat to medium low and simmer until tender, 30 to 35 minutes. Drain and rinse under cold water until easy to handle.

2. Meanwhile, warm the oil in a small saucepan over high heat until warm, about 1 minute. (Or microwave the oil in a microwavable bowl on high until the oil is warm, about 30 seconds.) Add the mint leaves and crush with handle of a wooden spoon or a pestle. Set aside.

3. Peel the sweet potatoes and return them to the saucepan. Add the mint mixture, lime juice, salt, and pepper. Mash with a potato masher until smooth and creamy. Transfer to a serving bowl, garnish with the mint sprigs, and serve hot.

nutty swiss chard

Like other dark leafy greens, Swiss chard is a nutritional powerhouse—a superb source of calcium and potassium, vitamin C, vitamin A and beta-carotene. I add cashews for texture and raisins for a hint of sweetness to the leaves and the stems.

MAKES 4 SERVINGS

1¼ pounds Swiss chard, well rinsed, stems chopped, leaves cut into 1-inch-thick slices

2 tablespoons olive oil

3 garlic cloves, thinly sliced

¼ cup golden raisins

¼ teaspoon kosher salt

¼ teaspoon freshly ground black pepper

¼ cup unsalted toasted cashews, chopped

1. Pull the chard stems from the leaves. Coarsely chop the stems, and cut the leaves crosswise into 1-inch-thick strips.

2. Heat the oil in a large nonstick skillet over medium heat. Add the stems and cook, stirring occasionally, until softened, about 10 minutes. Stir in the garlic and cook until fragrant, about 2 minutes. Stir in the leaves and cook, stirring often, until the leaves are tender, about 10 minutes. Stir in the raisins and season with salt and pepper. Transfer to a serving bowl and sprinkle with the cashews. Serve hot.

radicchio gratin

A fun and different way to have your veggies! Think of these radicchio leaves as a cross between kale chips (they will look charred) and potato skins. Whenever I make these, a few never make it to the table because I eat them in the kitchen!

MAKES 4 SERVINGS

cooking spray

vinaigrette:

2 tablespoons white balsamic vinegar

1 tablespoon olive oil

½ teaspoon kosher salt

¼ teaspoon freshly ground black pepper

1 head of radicchio, cut in half lengthwise, tough core removed

1 cup shredded *queso blanco*

¼ cup dried plain whole-wheat bread crumbs

2 tablespoons fresh basil leaves, finely chopped

1. Preheat the oven to 400°F. Spray a large baking sheet with olive oil cooking spray.

2. To make the vinaigrette, whisk together the vinegar, oil, salt, and pepper in a small bowl.

3. Separate the leaves from each half of the radicchio. Place the leaves on the baking sheet, overlapping them slightly. Brush both sides of the leaves with the vinaigrette. Bake until the leaves are wilted and slightly charred, about 10 minutes. Take out the leaves but leave the oven on.

4. Combine the cheese and bread crumbs in a medium bowl until well mixed. Sprinkle the cheese mixture evenly over the radicchio. Return to the oven and bake until the topping is golden brown and the cheese begins to melt slightly, about 8 minutes. Carefully transfer the radicchio to a platter and sprinkle with the basil. Serve warm or at room temperature.

anchovy-spiked broccoli

I don't blame you for hating anchovies if you've had only these salty fillets piled on pizza or draped over a salad. But I have the solution. Canned or jarred anchovies are best when they're mashed with other ingredients in a sauce or dressing like this combination of garlic, shallots, and sherry wine vinegar on broccoli.

MAKES 4 TO 6 SERVINGS

⅓ cup shallots, finely chopped

2 tablespoons sherry wine vinegar

2 tablespoons olive oil

4 flat anchovies in oil, drained and chopped

¼ teaspoon freshly ground black pepper

2 large broccoli heads, stems saved for another use, tops separated into florets

kosher salt

1. Combine the shallots, vinegar, 1 tablespoon of the oil, anchovies, and pepper in a large serving bowl until well mixed.

2. Heat the remaining 1 tablespoon of oil in a very large skillet over medium-high heat. Add the broccoli and cook, stirring occasionally, until the broccoli is bright green and crisp-tender, about 6 minutes. Transfer the broccoli to the bowl and toss well. Season with salt. Serve warm.

CHICA TIP

Anchovy paste in tubes is one of my favorite pantry ingredients. When I don't have any canned or jarred anchovies, I substitute ½ teaspoon anchovy paste for every two fillets. Add a touch to eggs, stews, sauces, and, of course, Caesar salad dressing. Once opened, the anchovy paste keeps indefinitely in the refrigerator.

crispy chickpeas, chorizo, and kale

A common trio in Portugal and Spain, chickpeas, chorizo, and kale make up a hearty side dish that can also be enjoyed as a main course.

MAKES 4 SERVINGS

1 tablespoon olive oil

1 15-ounce can garbanzo beans (chickpeas), rinsed, drained, and spread on a clean kitchen towel to thoroughly dry

½ cup (½-inch dice) hard, smoked Spanish-style chorizo

¼ cup golden raisins

1 pound kale, tough stems removed and leaves cut into 1-inch pieces

¼ cup reduced-sodium chicken broth

kosher salt

freshly ground black pepper

1. Heat a large skillet over medium-high heat for 2 minutes. Add the olive oil to the pan and allow to heat until shimmering but not smoking, about 30 seconds. Add the chickpeas and chorizo to the pan. Spread in a single layer so the beans make contact with the pan. Cover the skillet with a splatter screen (but not a lid) if you have one. Cook, stirring as little as possible, until the beans are crisp, about 15 minutes. Transfer to a bowl and stir in the raisins.

2. Reduce the heat to medium and stir in the kale. Add the broth and simmer until the kale is wilted, about 5 minutes. Season with salt and pepper. Transfer to a serving bowl and top with the bean mixture. Serve hot.

kale with oranges and shallots

Kale is another nutrient-packed dark leafy green that's finally getting the attention it deserves. I add orange juice and zest to brighten up its flavors. Try this with roast chicken or pork or stirred into quinoa for a vegetarian dinner.

MAKES 4 SERVINGS

2 tablespoons olive oil

½ cup shallots, finely chopped

¼ to ½ cup fresh orange juice

1 pound kale, tough stems removed and leaves roughly chopped

freshly grated zest of ¼ orange

1 large navel orange, cut into wedges, for garnish

In a large pan, heat the olive oil over medium heat. Sauté the shallots until soft (about 1 to 2 minutes); then add the orange juice. Stir ingredients to combine and start adding kale in batches (as you start stirring, it will begin reducing drastically). Once the kale is cooked to desired doneness, add the orange zest. Serve immediately, garnished with the fresh orange wedges.

CHICA TIP

I prefer kale when it still has a bit of crunch to it—almost al dente. If you like it more like sautéed spinach, add more orange juice and cook until soft and wilted.

spinach-and-mushroom-stuffed baked potatoes

Twice-baked potatoes are usually loaded with calories and fat, so I decided to come up with my own version of a fully loaded twice-baked potato using spinach and reduced-fat cheese. You'll never miss the other kind.

MAKES 8 SERVINGS

1 tablespoon olive oil

1 10-ounce package white mushrooms, chopped

1 small yellow onion, chopped

1 garlic clove, minced

2 tablespoons reduced-sodium chicken broth

1 teaspoon Worcestershire sauce

7 ounces baby spinach

4 large baking potatoes, about 12 ounces each, scrubbed but unpeeled

½ cup reduced-fat cheddar, shredded

cooking spray

½ cup low-fat or light sour cream

4 scallions, white and green parts, thinly sliced

1. Heat the oil in a large nonstick skillet over medium-high heat. Add the mushrooms, onion, and garlic and cook, stirring occasionally, until the vegetables are tender, about 8 minutes. Stir in the broth and Worcestershire sauce. Add the spinach in batches, and cook, stirring, until the spinach is wilted, about 5 minutes. Remove from the heat and set aside.

2. Meanwhile, wrap each potato in plastic wrap. Microwave on high until the potatoes are fork tender, 15 to 20 minutes. Cut the potatoes lengthwise in half. Scoop out some of the pulp into a large bowl, leaving a ¾-inch-thick border. Reserve the potato shells. Add the spinach mixture to the potato pulp in the bowl and mix well.

3. Position the broiler pan about 4 inches from the source of heat and preheat the broiler.

4. Spoon the spinach mixture evenly into the shells and sprinkle with the cheese. Spray the broiler pan with oil. Arrange the potatoes on the broiler pan and broil, 4 inches from the heat, until the filling is hot and the cheese is melted, 3 to 4 minutes. Remove from the broiler. Top each with a dollop of sour cream, sprinkle with scallions, and serve hot.

Indulge!
creamy chipotle mashed potatoes

If I'm going to indulge and eat mashed potatoes, then I want them to be as rich and creamy as possible. And that means adding butter, cream cheese, and milk. A hint of chipotle powder adds a chica touch. I prefer my mashed potatoes smooth and without any lumps. If you prefer them with a bit more texture, be my guest. After all, it's your indulgence.

MAKES 6 SERVINGS

2½ pounds red potatoes, peeled and cut into 1-inch pieces

1 8-ounce package cream cheese, cut into 1-inch pieces

½ cup milk

¼ cup unsalted butter, melted

1 teaspoon chipotle powder

½ teaspoon kosher salt

1. Place a steamer insert inside a large pot. Add 1½ inches of water and put the potatoes on the steamer insert. Bring to a boil, cover, and cook for 30 to 40 minute, until the potatoes are fork tender. Check periodically to make sure the water does not evaporate. Drain the potatoes in a colander and return them to the pot.

2. Add the cream cheese, milk, melted butter, chipotle powder, and salt. Using an electric hand mixer or a potato masher, mash the potatoes until smooth and creamy or to desired consistency.

hibiscus flower and ginger *agua fesca*
(*agua de jamaica*)

drinktastic!

When I want a cool, refreshing, and healthy beverage, I turn to my Latin American roots. I was always thirsty and starving by the time I got home from school for lunch, and my mother would give me a glass of homemade *agua fresca*, a blended drink of fresh fruits, flowers, or nuts with water and spices. Or when out with my family, we'd often stop for a frothy *batido*, a smoothie made with milk, fruit, and ice.

In towns and villages throughout Central and South America, people head to the treelined plazas in the afternoons to have an *agua fresca*, *batido*, or other beverage and catch up on the latest news and local gossip. Glasses of *horchata*, lemonade, hibiscus, or other colorful (and dairy-free) *aguas frescas* are ladled out from huge glass jars in restaurants and from street carts. At your next party, set out large containers with various *aguas frescas* and let guests serve themselves. *Batidos* can be made with berries, bananas, mango, papaya, pineapple, guava—just about any kind of fruit or fruit combination you can think of.

I frequently make myself a *batido*, using skim or almond milk, for a quick breakfast or an afternoon pick-me-up. To keep me energized, I add a scoop of protein powder as well.

key lime smoothies

Key lime pie is served in restaurants throughout southern Florida, where the small, tart yellow limes are grown. I wanted a smoothie with those same flavors, but Key limes can be hard to find in many places. Made with Persian limes, these smoothies have all the flavors of a slice of Key lime pie but with far fewer calories.

MAKES 2 SERVINGS

1 cup ice cubes

½ cup cold water

1 2.7-ounce container nonfat plain Greek yogurt

stevia or preferred sweetener, to taste

freshly grated zest of ¼ lime

1 tablespoon fresh lime juice

¼ teaspoon vanilla extract

lime wedge, for garnish

Puree the ice cubes, water, yogurt, stevia, lime zest, lime juice, and vanilla in a blender until smooth. Pour into a tall glass, garnish with the lime wedge, and serve immediately.

CHICA TIP

Batidos, shakes, and other smoothies are best when they're served really cold. Cold ingredients are essential, but I also chill the blender jar and serving glasses in the freezer for ten minutes before making these drinks.

drinktastic!

mango-mint fizz

While I was growing up, we had a beautiful mango tree in the garden, and I learned to use the fruit in endless ways. Here, mango and mint join forces with tart lemonade to beat the heat on a hot day. Mango also adds an exotic fruity flavor and brings in that tropical feel to this summer drink. I sweeten it with a touch of honey and add sparkling water for a fizzy, refreshing drink.

MAKES 4 SERVINGS

1 cup ice cubes

1 cup mango puree, homemade or frozen, thawed

¼ cup fresh lime juice

2 tablespoons honey

6 to 8 fresh mint leaves

2 cups club soda

lime wedges, for garnish

fresh mint sprigs, for garnish

1. Blend the ice cubes, mango puree, lime juice, honey, and mint leaves together in a blender until almost smooth, about 30 seconds—the small chunks of ice are refreshing.

2. Pour into glasses, top with sparkling water, garnish with lime wedges and mint sprigs, and serve immediately.

drinktastic!

cocadas in a glass

Cocadas, chewy, soft coconut-vanilla-cinnamon candies or cookies, are popular throughout Latin America, where they're sold from street carts or by peddlers on beaches. I use those same confectionary flavors to make these *batidos*.

MAKES 4 SERVINGS

1½ cups 2% reduced-fat or skim milk

1 cup sweetened coconut flakes

3 cups ice cubes

1 teaspoon vanilla extract

1 teaspoon coconut extract

1 teaspoon ground cinnamon

Blend the milk and coconut in a blender until smooth, about 1 minute. Add the ice cubes, vanilla, coconut extract, and cinnamon, and blend until slushy, about 1 minute more. Pour into chilled glasses and serve immediately.

tamarind-papaya spritzers

When my grandmother came to visit us in the Caribbean, the first thing she did was pick some pods from our tamarind tree. She boiled them to make a tart juice that she drank every morning, insisting it kept her slim. My father had his own morning ritual: eating sliced papaya with a squirt of lemon at breakfast. I decided to combine both family breakfast flavors in this sweet-and-sour spritzer, but you can enjoy this refreshing drink any time of the day.

MAKES 2 TO 3 SERVINGS

1 cup frozen tamarind pulp, thawed

½ cup canned papaya nectar

2 tablespoons fresh lemon juice

stevia or preferred sweetener, to taste

ice cubes, for serving

1 cup ginger ale, as needed

lemon wedges, for garnish

1. Blend the tamarind pulp, papaya nectar, lemon juice, and stevia to taste in a blender until combined and frothy, about 1 minute.

2. Pour equal amounts of the tamarind mixture into ice-filled glasses. Top each with ginger ale. Garnish each with a lemon wedge and serve immediately.

drinktastic!

vitamin c overload

My sisters and I always made this drink when we visited my grandparents. The flavor and color are beautiful from the combination of tomatoes and oranges. They are rich in vitamin C, but also provide vitamin A, which is good for healthy skin, hair, and eyes. Whenever I feel a cold coming on, I make myself a batch of Vitamin C Overload.

1⅓ cups fresh orange juice (from 3 large oranges)

2 Roma tomatoes

2 tablespoons fresh lime juice

2 tablespoons honey

celery sticks, for garnish

Blend the orange juice, tomatoes, lime juice, and honey in a blender until smooth. Pour into glasses, garnish with celery sticks, and serve immediately.

vida green juice

Drinking a glass of green juice is the best way I can think of to get all the nutrition and goodness from vegetables. Making tasty green juices can be a challenge, but apple slices and a knob of ginger add blasts of flavor. Keep a stash of cleaned and ready-to-go vegetables in your refrigerator to put this drink together in no time. To make this drink, you will need to purchase a centrifugal juicer.

MAKES 2 SERVINGS

2 apples, sliced

3 carrots, peeled

3 celery stalks

3 cups packed spinach leaves, including stems

1 large bunch of parsley, including stems

1 2-inch piece of fresh ginger, unpeeled

1 English cucumber, unpeeled

Wash all the produce well. Pass through a centrifugal juicer. Pour into glasses and serve immediately.

rice cooler (*horchata*)

Horchata is a thirst-quenching drink made from finely ground rice combined with vanilla, almonds, and cinnamon. *Horchata* is served from huge glass jars in bodegas or from food carts and trucks throughout the United States, Mexico, and Central America. It's often referred to as "the drink of the gods" for its rich flavor. It's the best way to cool off on a hot summer's day.

MAKES 4 TO 6 SERVINGS

1 quart warm water

1 cup raw long-grain white rice

½ cup 2% reduced-fat milk

2 teaspoons vanilla extract

½ teaspoon almond extract

½ teaspoon ground cinnamon

stevia or preferred sweetener, to taste

ice cubes, for serving

whole cinnamon sticks, for serving (optional)

1. Process the warm water and rice in a blender until it is coarsely ground but not mushy, 1 to 2 minutes. Refrigerate in the blender jar for at least 6 hours and up to 12 hours.

2. Strain the rice mixture through a fine-mesh wire sieve and discard the rice in the sieve. (If the rice passes through the sieve, line the sieve with several layers of rinsed cheesecloth.) Reserve the rice water.

3. Blend the rice water, milk, vanilla, almond extract, cinnamon, and stevia until well combined. Pour the *horchata* into ice-filled glasses and add cinnamon sticks to use as stirrers, if desired.

latin d'lite

hibiscus flower and ginger *agua fresca* (agua de jamaica)

Jamaica (ha-MAY-kuh), or hibiscus, flowers create one of the most stunning and delicious infusions you can imagine. In Mexico, this drink is as popular as iced tea is in the States. I add some ginger to mine for another layer of flavor. Serve this jewellike ruby red and slightly tart juice well-chilled and over ice.

4 cups water

4 bags of hibiscus tea, such as Badia brand

6 fresh mint leaves

½ teaspoon stevia or preferred sweetener

2 tablespoons fresh ginger, peeled and shredded

2 tablespoons fresh lemon juice

ice cubes, for serving

4 lemon wedges, for garnish

4 fresh mint sprigs, for garnish

1. Bring the water to a boil in a medium saucepan over high heat. Remove from the heat and add the hibiscus tea and mint leaves. Let stand 5 minutes. Using a slotted spoon, remove the tea bags, pressing hard on the bags.

2. Transfer to a heatproof pitcher and stir in the stevia, ginger, and lemon juice. Refrigerate until chilled, at least 4 hours.

3. Pour into 4 ice-filled glasses, garnish each with a lemon wedge and mint sprig, and serve immediately.

pineapple-cucumber *agua fresca*

The combination of pineapple and cucumber with some basil reminds me of the refreshing and cleansing waters served at many spas after a workout or a massage.

MAKES 6 SERVINGS

2 cups water

2 cups pineapple, pared, cored, and chopped

1 cup cucumber, peeled, seeded, and chopped

2 tablespoons fresh basil leaves, chopped

6 large basil leaves, for garnish

Puree the water, pineapple, cucumber, and chopped basil in a blender. Pour into 6 glasses, garnish each with a basil leaf, and serve immediately.

minty melonade

I can't think of anything more refreshing than this combination of honeydew melon and lime juice. It's finished with a splash of sparkling water, and just looking at this drink will cool you off.

MAKES 4 TO 6 SERVINGS

1 very ripe honeydew melon, peeled, seeded, and diced

½ cup fresh lime juice

6 fresh mint leaves

club soda, as needed

fresh mint sprigs, for garnish

Puree the melon, lime juice, and mint leaves in a blender. Pour equal amounts into glasses. Top each with a splash of club soda and garnish with a mint sprig. Serve immediately.

drinktastic!

Indulge!
chocolate blitz shake

When I have a craving for something rich and chocolaty, I whip up this delicious shake. I add some frozen M&M's to the blender for a candy kick. Pour the mixture into tall glasses and serve for dessert after a barbecue or while watching a movie. It's truly worth the indulgence!

1 1.3-ounce milk chocolate bar, broken into small pieces

1½ cups vanilla ice cream

½ cup whole milk

1 teaspoon almond extract

pinch of ground cinnamon

1 cup candy-covered dark chocolate, such as M&M's, frozen

1. Chill a blender jar and 4 serving glasses in the freezer.

2. Place the milk chocolate bar in a microwave-safe bowl. Using the defrost setting, microwave for 1 to 2 minutes, stirring every 30 seconds, until melted. Let cool until tepid.

3. Blend the ice cream, milk, melted chocolate, almond extract, and cinnamon in the chilled blender jar until smooth. Add the frozen candy and pulse several times to chop into small bits. Pour into the chilled glasses and serve immediately with spoons.

santa nick's naughty punch

cocktailicious— drink up your calories, chica!

I often joke that I'd rather drink my calories than eat them, so it's no wonder that I'm well-known for my cocktails. This is definitely my indulgence chapter!

When entertaining my friends at home, I often greet them at the door with a signature drink created just for that evening's dinner or weekend brunch. I set up a bar with all the makings—and the recipe—of the cocktail so they can make it themselves after the first round. That way I can tend to the finishing touches in the kitchen. By serving one unique cocktail at a party, you don't need a fully stocked bar. (And all the money I don't spend on liquor goes into my shoe fund!)

Cocktails should be fun and well balanced—never too sweet, never too tart. One ingredient should never overpower any other flavors. These are fun, sophisticated, yet easy homemade cocktails.

Living a healthy lifestyle isn't about giving everything up; it's about finding a balance. You can always treat yourself; just make sure you do so in moderation. And a word of caution: Don't drink and drive.

cherrylicious

Keep a jar of macerated cherries—fruit soaked in alcohol—in your refrigerator to make this cocktail on the spur of the moment. I fill a glass jar with frozen pitted cherries and add enough rum to cover. The longer you let the cherries sit in the rum, the better. You'll find plenty of other uses for them—a topping for frozen yogurt or add some to a bottle of vinegar. For a sweet treat, save some of those frozen cherries to eat right from the bag.

MAKES 6 SERVINGS

macerated cherries:

1 12-ounce bag frozen cherries

1 cup silver rum

½ cup sugar

¾ cup silver rum

¾ cup orange-flavored liqueur, such as triple sec or Grand Marnier

¼ cup syrup from macerated cherries

¼ cup fresh lime juice

ice cubes

2 cups sparkling water

18 macerated cherries, for serving

6 fresh lime zest curls, removed with a "channel" citrus zester, for garnish

1. To make the macerated cherries, stir the cherries, rum, and sugar to dissolve the sugar. Cover and refrigerate for at least 30 minutes. (The cherries will keep, covered and refrigerated, for up to 2 months.)

2. Stir the rum, liqueur, syrup, and lime juice together in a large pitcher. Add ice cubes and stir well to chill. Add the sparkling water and stir gently.

3. For each serving, put 3 macerated cherries in the bottom of a champagne flute and pour in the chilled liquid. Garnish with a lime curl.

CHICA TIP

> Fill an ice cube tray with lemonade, place a macerated cherry in each indentation, and then freeze. Use in cocktails, lemonade, or iced tea.

pink *caipirinha*

"I believe in pink," starts an inspirational quote by actress Audrey Hepburn. Well, I do too! And this is the pinkest drink ever. I add a touch of pomegranate liqueur to Brazil's national cocktail, the *Caipirinha*. This pink cocktail is just the ticket for a girls' night in.

MAKES 4 SERVINGS

4 limes, each cut into eighths

½ cup sugar

1 cup *cachaça* (Brazilian sugarcane rum)

¼ cup pomegranate liqueur

crushed ice or ice cubes

lime wedges, for garnish

1. Using a pestle (from a mortar and pestle), a cocktail muddler, or the end of a wooden spoon, muddle the limes and sugar in a large covered container (a jar works well). Add the *cachaça* and the liqueur and shake well.

2. Pour over ice in rocks glasses, garnish with lime wedges, and serve immediately.

CHICA TIP

! Replace the *cachaça* with an equal amount of rum for a *Caipirissima* or with vodka for a *Caipiroska*. More pink cocktails!

cocktailicous—drink up your calories, chica!

blood orange beer cocktail

A *refajo*, a popular cocktail in Colombia, is made by mixing beer with *Colombiana*, a cola-flavored soda. It's often accompanied by a shot of *aguardiente*, the country's national liquor. I sometimes pop open a cold beer on a hot, blistering Miami day. But when I want a cocktail that takes me home, I make a *refajo* with beer, tequila, and blood orange sorbet. An extra shot of tequila is entirely up to you.

1 lime, quartered

1 cup blood orange sorbet

¾ cup silver tequila

4 12-ounce bottles light beer, chilled

4 blood orange or orange rounds, for garnish

For each serving, squeeze the juice of 1 lime quarter into a tall glass. Add 1 scoop (about ¼ cup) sorbet and 3 tablespoons of tequila and mix with a long spoon. In two stages, letting the foam subside between pours, carefully fill the glass with beer. Garnish with an orange round. Serve immediately.

cocktailicous—drink up your calories, chica!

spiked chica iced tea

I always keep a pitcher of iced tea in the refrigerator. When I come home from a long day at work, all I have to do is muddle some lime and sugar in a tall glass and add some passion fruit nectar and dark rum for my favorite summer drink. Passion fruit is not only high in antioxidants, but is widely used to relax the body and mind. So sit back, de-stress, and enjoy!

1 family-size bag iced tea or 4 regular bags black tea

4 cups boiling water

4 limes, quartered

¾ cup sugar

1 cup passion fruit nectar

½ cup dark rum

ice cubes

4 lime rounds

1. Put the ice tea bag(s) in a heatproof iced tea jar or pitcher. Pour in the boiling water and let steep for 5 to 8 minutes. The tea should be very strong.

2. Meanwhile, using a pestle (from a mortar and pestle), a cocktail muddler, or the end of a wooden spoon, muddle the limes and sugar together in a heatproof medium bowl.

3. Pour the hot brewed tea over the lime mixture, pressing hard on the tea bags. Stir well to dissolve the sugar. Stir in the passion fruit nectar and rum. Stir until blended. To serve, pour over ice in tall glasses and garnish with lime rounds.

mango cava bellini

I put my Latina spin on the Venetian Bellini of peach puree and prosecco by using mango puree and cava. Bright and fresh, this burst of bubbly is a welcome addition to any brunch! Cava is a sparkling white or rosé wine from Spain. Cava is underrated, unknown, and underpriced. Once you try cava, you'll say good-bye to those costly French champagnes. Many cavas are even made from the same grape as high-end champagnes.

2 mangoes, pitted, peeled, and coarsely chopped

1 750-ml bottle dry cava, chilled

1. Puree the mango in a blender.

2. For each serving, pour 2 tablespoons of mango puree into a champagne flute. In two stages, letting the foam subside between pours, carefully fill the glasses with cava.

cocktailicous—drink up your calories, chica!

mandarin orange champagne cocktail

Is it a cocktail? Or is it dessert? It's both! I blend lemon sorbet with vodka and mandarin oranges, pour the mixture into tall or margarita glasses, and then add a splash of champagne.

MAKES 4 SERVINGS

2 cups lemon sorbet

½ cup canned mandarin oranges, drained and rinsed

½ cup vodka

¼ cup champagne or sparkling wine

fresh mint sprigs, for garnish

Puree the sorbet, oranges, and vodka in a blender. Divide the mixture among 4 tall glasses. Top each with a splash (about 1 tablespoon) of champagne, garnish with the mint, and serve immediately.

beloved whiskey

Scotch and other whiskeys are popular throughout South America. While beer is my first beverage choice, I also like a good pour of Scotch on the rocks. It never occurred to me to mix it with other ingredients until I came to America. When I decided to play around and create some cocktails, I was pleasantly surprised to see how well Scotch goes with herbs and other mixers.

MAKES 2 SERVINGS

mint syrup:

½ cup sugar

½ cup water

¼ cup packed fresh mint leaves

6 tablespoons Scotch

2 teaspoons Mint Syrup

1 tablespoon fresh lime juice

ice cubes

¾ cup ginger ale

fresh mint sprigs, for garnish

lime rounds, for garnish

1. To make the mint syrup, bring the sugar and water to a boil in a small saucepan over medium-high heat, stirring until the sugar dissolves. Remove from the heat and add the mint. Cool completely. Strain the syrup into a small covered container, pressing hard on the mint. (The syrup will keep, covered and refrigerated, for up to 2 months.)

2. Shake the whiskey, Mint Syrup, and lime juice in a cocktail shaker with ice until well chilled and combined. Add the ginger ale and stir gently.

3. Strain into ice-filled glasses. Garnish with the mint and lime rounds and serve.

raspberry passiontini

No need to wait for Valentine's Day to enjoy this sexy cocktail made with raspberry vodka, passion fruit pulp, rosemary-infused simple syrup, and a splash of ginger ale.

MAKES 2 SERVINGS

rosemary syrup:

½ cup sugar

½ cup water

3 3-inch fresh rosemary sprigs

4 ounces black raspberry vodka, chilled

¼ cup passion fruit pulp (available in the frozen section of Latino markets)

½ cup Rosemary Syrup, chilled

ice cubes

6 ounces ginger ale, chilled

2 fresh raspberries, for garnish

2 3-inch-long rosemary sprigs, for garnish

1. To make the rosemary syrup, bring the sugar and water to a boil in a small saucepan over medium-high heat, stirring until the sugar dissolves. Remove from the heat and add the rosemary. Let stand for 30 minutes. Strain the syrup into a small covered container, pressing hard on the rosemary. Refrigerate until chilled, at least 4 hours. (The syrup will keep, covered and refrigerated, for up to 2 months.)

2. Shake the vodka, passion fruit pulp, and Rosemary Syrup in a cocktail mixer with ice until well chilled and combined. Strain into 2 large martini glasses. Top each with ginger ale.

3. Skewer each raspberry with a rosemary sprig (you may have to remove some of the leaves from the bottom of the stem to do so), and place a skewer in each glass. Serve immediately.

pineapple melontini

Midori, which means green in Japanese, is a sweet, melon-flavored liqueur. Just a touch of this bright green liqueur balances the flavors in this summery pineapple-vodka cocktail.

½ cup orange-flavored vodka

¼ cup pineapple juice

¼ cup Midori

ice cubes

¾ cup lemon-lime soda, chilled

fresh pineapple chunks, for garnish

2 3-inch wooden skewers, for garnish

1. Shake the orange-flavored vodka, pineapple juice, and Midori in a cocktail mixer with ice until well chilled and combined.

2. Divide between 2 martini glasses and top each with the soda. Thread the pineapple onto the skewers and use to garnish the drinks. Serve immediately.

cocktailicous—drink up your calories, chica!

santa nick's naughty punch

When actor/rapper Nick Cannon and I threw a holiday party, he asked me to create a signature punch for our guests. Apples and ginger say Christmas, so I paired them with vodka, white wine, and champagne. How naughty and nice for a partying crowd.

MAKES 12 TO 14 SERVINGS

1 cup sugar

2 cups ginger-flavored vodka

1 pound sweet apples, such as Red Gala, cored and cut into 1-inch dice

1 750-ml bottle champagne or sparkling wine, chilled

1 bottle dry white wine, such as pinot grigio

1 quart apple juice, chilled

1. Whisk the sugar and the vodka together in a large bowl. Pour into a resealable plastic bag, add the apples, close, and refrigerate for at least 8 hours and up to 1 day.

2. Pour the apples and their soaking liquid into a large punch bowl. Add the champagne, wine, and apple juice. Serve, ladling some diced apples into each glass.

CHICA TIP

To keep punch from becoming watered down, pour apple juice into a round mold and freeze. Add it to the bowl, once the punch is mixed.

cocktailicous—drink up your calories, chica!

mexican sangria

Traditional Spanish sangria is made with red or white wine and some brandy, sugar, fruit, and sparkling water. But since I'm a chica who loves to play with tradition in the kitchen, I came up with this white wine and tequila sangria. If your friends are like mine, you'll probably have to double the recipe.

MAKES 8 SERVINGS

1 cup seedless green grapes

1 cup silver tequila

1 750-ml bottle dry white wine, such as pinot grigio

1½ cups bottled white grape juice

¼ cup fresh lime juice

2 tablespoons superfine sugar

2 limes, each cut into eighths

1 quart sparkling water, plus extra for serving ice, for serving

lime rounds, for garnish

1. Combine the grapes and tequila in a large pitcher. Let stand for 1 hour.

2. Add the wine, grape juice, lime juice, sugar, and limes and stir to dissolve the sugar. Add the sparkling water and stir gently. Pour into ice-filled glasses, and top each with additional sparkling water, if desired. Garnish with the lime rounds and serve.

coconut *gingerito*

Ginger beer is a nonspicy but zippy carbonated beverage that's popular throughout the Caribbean. I decided to create a cocktail with two other tropical favorites—coconut and rum—and came up with this delicious concoction.

¼ cup sweetened coconut flakes

1 large lime wedge

¾ cup coconut-flavored rum

3 tablespoons cream of coconut, such as Coco Lopez

¼ cup packed fresh cilantro

8 fresh mint leaves

8 fresh basil leaves

¼ cup fresh lime juice

crushed ice

ginger beer, chilled, for serving

fresh mint sprigs, for garnish

1. Preheat the oven to 350°F. Spread the coconut on a rimmed baking sheet. Bake, stirring occasionally, until lightly browned, about 10 minutes. Let cool completely. Pulse in a food processor or blender until finely crushed.

2. Moisten the edge of 4 martini glasses by rubbing with the lime wedge. Spread the coconut in a saucer. Roll the outer edge only of each glass in the coconut to coat it.

3. Combine the rum, cream of coconut, cilantro, mint, and basil in a cocktail shaker. Using a pestle (from a mortar and pestle), a cocktail muddler, or the end of a wooden spoon, muddle the herbs with the other ingredients. Add the lime juice and ice, and shake until well chilled and combined.

4. Fill each prepared glass with crushed ice. Strain equal amounts of the rum mixture into the glasses. Top each with ginger beer and garnish with a mint sprig. Serve immediately.

mini mango-lemongrass-passion fruit trifles

happy endings

When it comes to desserts, I'm picky. I like desserts that are quick to put together and have just a touch of sweetness. I generally prefer fruity desserts, but, like most chicas, I find there are days when I have to have my chocolate or some other sweet indulgence!

Being healthy doesn't mean giving up desserts forever. The secret is to enjoy them in moderation. That's easier said than done if you're someone who loves sweets! The good news is that this chapter features recipes that satisfy your sweet tooth and maintain your waistline. When grilled, pineapple and other fruits become even sweeter and more succulent. For easy preparation and stunning presentation, store-bought angel food cake can be drizzled with a lemongrass–passion fruit syrup and layered with mango and yogurt. When it comes to throwing all caution to the wind, it's time for *sopapillas*, those puffy, warm-from-the-oil Mexican doughnuts drizzled with honey or dusted with sugar.

raspberry-ricotta-yogurt *granita*

Granitas remind me of the *raspados*, snow cones with crazy-colored fruit syrups, sold on the streets in Colombia when I was a child. Instead of shaved ice, I shave some frozen fruit-flavored yogurt into bowls and top them with creamy ricotta whipped with honey and orange zest.

MAKES 4 SERVINGS

3 6-ounce containers "light" fat-free raspberry yogurt

½ cup part-skim ricotta cheese

2 teaspoons honey

freshly grated zest of 1 orange

fresh raspberries, for garnish

1. Spread the yogurt in an 8-inch-square metal baking dish and cover with plastic wrap. Freeze until just frozen, about 1 hour.

2. Using the tines of a fork, scrape the frozen yogurt into ice flakes. Cover again and return to the freezer and freeze for another 30 minutes. Repeat freezing and scraping at 30-minute intervals until the yogurt is flaky and fluffy, about 2 hours total.

3. Whisk the ricotta, honey, and orange zest together in a small bowl. Transfer to a small zip-tight plastic bag and squeeze the ricotta into a corner of the bag. Snip off the corner with scissors to make a piping bag.

4. Spoon equal amounts of the *granita* into 4 chilled small dessert glasses. Pipe each with the ricotta mixture and garnish with the raspberries. Serve immediately.

mango sorbet infused with rosewater

Welcome to my world of sorbets made without an ice-cream machine! I blend lime syrup with frozen mango, some dry white wine, and a hint of rosewater for a light, floral flavor. Once the mixture is frozen, serve scoops in your prettiest glasses. Instead of the mango, you can substitute strawberries, peaches, pineapple, or any combination of your favorite fruits.

MAKES ABOUT 1 QUART, 4 TO 6 SERVINGS

lime syrup:

1 cup sugar

¾ cup water

freshly grated zest of 1 lime

3 ripe mangoes, cut into chunks and frozen, or 2 cups frozen mango pieces

2 cups ice cubes

½ cup dry white wine, such as pinot grigio

1 teaspoon rosewater

fresh mint sprigs, for garnish

1. To make the lime syrup, bring the sugar, water, and lime zest to a boil in a small saucepan over medium heat, stirring until the sugar dissolves. Reduce the heat to low and simmer for 1 minute, being sure the syrup is smooth. Remove from the heat and let cool completely.

2. Puree the cooled syrup with the frozen mango chunks, ice, wine, and rosewater in a food processor until the ice has broken down and the mixture is slushy, about 2 minutes. Transfer the sorbet to an airtight container, cover, and freeze until hard enough to hold its shape, at least 1 hour. (The sorbet can be frozen for up to 2 weeks.)

3. To serve, spoon into chilled martini glasses and garnish with mint sprigs. Serve frozen.

CHICA TIP

Rosewater, a clear fragrant water made by distilling rose petals, is popular in North African, Middle Eastern, and Latin sweet and savory dishes. A little goes a long way; use it sparingly or your food will taste bitter. Rosewater will keep indefinitely in a cool, dark place.

cup o' baked spiced hot chocolate

Chocolate lovers, this will become a favorite. It has many different chocolate layers and textures and far fewer calories than chocolate mousse or other desserts. The outer layer is dry, almost brownie-like, while the inside oozes with molten chocolate. Just writing about it makes my mouth water!

MAKES 4 SERVINGS

9 ounces bittersweet chocolate, coarsely chopped (you can also use chips or chunks)

6 tablespoons (¾ stick) unsalted butter, cut into tablespoons

½ teaspoon chili powder

¼ teaspoon ground cinnamon

4 large eggs, at room temperature

¼ cup sugar

light whipped cream, for serving

1. Preheat the oven to 350°F.

2. Melt the chocolate and butter together in a heatproof medium bowl placed over a medium saucepan of barely simmering water over low heat, stirring occasionally. (The bottom of the bowl should not touch the water.) Remove the bowl from the heat and stir in the chili powder and cinnamon.

3. Whisk the eggs and sugar in another heatproof medium bowl until combined. Place over the simmering water in the saucepan and beat until the egg mixture is warm to the touch (wash your fingers well with soap and water before and after testing the temperature), about 1 minute. Remove from the heat. With an electric hand mixer on high speed, beat the egg mixture until light and fluffy and more than doubled in volume, 2 to 3 minutes.

4. Pour the egg mixture over the chocolate mixture and fold together with a rubber spatula. Ladle or pour into 4 5- to 6-ounce ramekins or oven-safe coffee cups. Fold a kitchen towel to fit flat inside of a 9 × 13-inch baking pan. Arrange the ramekins on the towel. Put the baking dish in the oven, and slide it out on the rack. Carefully pour enough hot water to come halfway up the sides of the ramekins; then carefully slide the rack with the baking dish back into the oven.

5. Bake until the tops look crusty, 15 to 20 minutes. Remove the pan from the oven. Place each ramekin on a serving dish, top with a dollop of whipped cream, and serve immediately.

happy endings

grilled pineapple with spiked rum crema

Have you ever grilled pineapple or other fruits? If not, you're in for a real treat. The heat caramelizes the fruit, intensifying its sweet tropical flavor. Serve the pineapple with a spoonful of rum-laced whipped cream or a scoop of frozen yogurt for an easy summer dessert. The only thing better than grilled pineapple would be a platter of grilled mixed fruits, such as peaches, nectarines, bananas, mangoes, or papaya.

MAKES 4 SERVINGS

8 ¾-inch-thick rounds of pineapple, peeled and cored

butter-flavored cooking spray

3 tablespoons dark brown sugar

1 cup heavy cream

½ cup confectioners' sugar

2 tablespoons silver rum

¼ cup sweetened coconut flakes, toasted, for serving

fresh mint sprigs, for garnish

1. Spray the pineapple slices with the cooking spray on both sides and rub with the dark brown sugar.

2. Beat the heavy cream with an electric hand mixer on high speed in a chilled medium bowl until it thickens. Add the confectioners' sugar and beat until stiff peaks form. Beat in the rum until stiff peaks form. Refrigerate until ready to serve.

3. Heat a rimmed grill pan over high heat until very hot. In batches, add the pineapple to the pan and grill until seared with grill marks, turning once, about 3 minutes. (The pineapple can also be grilled on an outdoor grill over medium heat.) Transfer to a plate and let cool slightly.

4. For each serving, place 2 pineapple slices on a dessert plate. Top with a dollop of the rum cream, sprinkle with a tablespoon of coconut, and garnish with a mint sprig. Serve immediately.

happy endings

chocolate-oatmeal cookies

I use unsweetened applesauce and a touch of honey to replace half of the sugar in these chewy oatmeal cookies. But you won't feel deprived, since there are cinnamony-chocolate chips in every bite.

MAKES ABOUT 2 DOZEN

½ cup unsweetened applesauce

½ cup sugar (or any granular natural sweetener)

1 large egg

1 teaspoon vanilla extract

1 tablespoon honey

1 tablespoon olive oil

1 cup whole-wheat flour, sifted

1½ cups old-fashioned (rolled) oats

½ teaspoon baking powder

½ teaspoon baking soda

½ teaspoon table salt

1 tablespoon ground cinnamon

½ cup semisweet chocolate chips

1. Position racks in the top and lower thirds of the oven and preheat to 350°F.

2. Mix the applesauce and sugar together in a medium bowl with an electric hand mixer on high speed until well combined, about 1 minute. Add the egg, vanilla, honey, and olive oil and mix well.

3. In a bowl, mix together the flour, oats, baking powder, baking soda, salt, and cinnamon. Slowly add the oat mixture to the applesauce mixture and mix just until combined. Add the chocolate chips, and mix.

4. Using a regular teaspoon, drop teaspoonfuls of cookie dough onto two parchment-lined rimmed baking sheets, leaving at least 2 inches between cookies. Bake until browned and crispy around the edges, switching the pans halfway through, about 14 to 16 minutes. Let cool on wire racks.

spiced strawberries and crema

It may sound odd, but balsamic vinegar actually does bring out the inherent sweetness of fresh strawberries. I add a hint of allspice to the mixture and top each serving with a dollop of whipped cream and some chocolate shavings for another quick, light, and winning dessert.

MAKES 4 SERVINGS

1½ pounds strawberries, hulled and quartered

1½ tablespoons white balsamic vinegar

2 .035-ounce packets stevia

pinch ground allspice

1 cup heavy cream

½ cup confectioners' sugar

1 1.30-ounce bar dark chocolate with almonds

1. Mix the strawberries, white balsamic vinegar, stevia, and allspice in a medium bowl. Let rest for 20 minutes.

2. To make whipped cream, beat the heavy cream with an electric hand mixer on high speed in a chilled medium bowl until it thickens. Add the confectioners' sugar and beat until stiff peaks form. Refrigerate until ready to serve.

3. Divide among 4 dessert bowls and top with a dollop of whipped cream. Using a swivel vegetable peeler, shave the chocolate over the berries and cream, and serve at once.

banana-almond bread pudding

Heavy and dense bread pudding is the last thing I want to eat after a great meal, so I decided it was time to lighten up this classic dessert. Mine uses honey-wheat bread, almond milk, and very ripe bananas with a touch of spiced rum for a more delicate and waistline-friendly treat.

MAKES 6 TO 8 SERVINGS

cooking spray

4 cups vanilla-flavored almond milk

4 large eggs

½ cup packed light brown sugar

3 ripe bananas, 1 mashed and 2 sliced into ½-inch-thick rounds

2 tablespoons spiced rum

½ teaspoon ground cinnamon

½ teaspoon vanilla extract

pinch of table salt

12 slices honey-wheat bread, cut into 1-inch-square pieces

¼ cup dark raisins

½ cup natural almonds, sliced

1. Preheat the oven to 375°F. Spray a 9 × 13-inch baking dish with oil.

2. Whisk the almond milk, eggs and sugar together in a large bowl. Whisk in the mashed banana, rum, cinnamon, vanilla, and salt. Add bread, raisins, and sliced bananas. Stir gently and let stand for 5 minutes, making sure the bread soaks up some of the liquid. Spread evenly into the baking dish. Sprinkle the almonds on top.

3. Bake until the pudding is slightly puffed and feels set when lightly pressed in the center with a fingertip, about 40 minutes. Let cool for 15 to 30 minutes. Spoon into bowls and serve warm.

mini mango-lemongrass–passion fruit trifles

A trifle is usually made with rum- or brandy-soaked ladyfingers or sponge cake layered in a large glass bowl with berries and whipped cream or custard. This chica layers rounds of store-bought angel food cake, lemongrass–passion fruit syrup, mango, and yogurt in eight short glasses about three inches wide for an elegant finish to any dinner.

MAKES 8 SERVINGS

lemongrass–passion fruit syrup:

- 1 lemongrass stalk, hard outer layers removed, and soft center crushed
- 1 cup water
- ½ cup sugar
- ¼ cup frozen passion fruit pulp, thawed
- 1 cup 2% low-fat plain Greek yogurt
- 2 .035-ounce packets stevia or your preferred sweetener
- 1 store-bought angel food cake
- 2 mangoes (not too ripe), peeled, pitted, and cut into ¼-inch cubes
- zest of 1 lime, for garnish

1. To prepare the syrup, start by trimming the lemongrass. Cut off the tough bottom tip and top of the stalk where it meets the more tender bulbous part. Slice a lengthwise slit in the lemongrass, and remove the tough outer layers until you reach the softer inner bulb. On the cutting board, smash the lemongrass underneath the flat side of a chef's knife; then chop it finely.

2. Bring the lemongrass, water, and sugar to a boil in a small saucepan over medium heat, stirring until the sugar dissolves. Boil briskly for 5 minutes; then reduce the heat to medium low and simmer until the syrup has thickened lightly, about 5 minutes. Let cool and add passion fruit pulp.

3. Mix the yogurt and stevia in a small bowl until combined. Cover and refrigerate until ready to use.

4. Cut the cake into 1-inch-thick slices. Using a 3-inch-diameter metal biscuit cutter or ring mold, cut out 16 rounds.

5. Have ready 8 small dessert dishes about 3 inches wide. For each trifle, place a cake round in a glass. Drizzle with 1 teaspoon of the syrup, a few mango cubes, and 1 tablespoon of yogurt. Repeat. Grate the lime zest over the top of each trifle. Cover each glass with plastic wrap and refrigerate until chilled, at least 1 hour and up to 8 hours.

rosewater raspberry *merenguitos*

A bit of raspberry gelatin gives these pillowy low-fat meringues their delicate pink color. Rosewater adds a gentle, flowery taste to the cookies. Serve these sweets as an accompaniment to sorbet at a bridal shower or other girly party.

MAKES 5 DOZEN

cooking spray

3 large egg whites, at room temperature

¼ teaspoon table salt

¾ cup sugar

1½ tablespoons raspberry-flavored gelatin powder, such as Jell-O

½ teaspoon rosewater

¼ teaspoon distilled white vinegar

1. Position racks in the upper third and center of the oven and preheat to 250°F. Spray 2 large baking sheets with cooking spray (to help secure the parchment) and line with parchment paper.

2. Whip the egg whites and salt together in a large, grease-free bowl with an electric hand mixer set on high speed until they form soft peaks. Gradually beat in the sugar and raspberry gelatin powder and beat until the mixture forms stiff, shiny peaks. Fold in the rosewater and vinegar.

3. Transfer the meringue to a pastry bag fitted with a ½-inch-wide star tip. Spacing them about 1 inch apart, pipe 1-inch-wide meringues onto the lined baking sheets. Bake until the meringues look set, about 1 hour. Turn the oven off, and let the meringues completely cool and dry in the oven. Carefully lift the meringues off the parchment and store in an airtight container.

chocolate-dipped apricots

These simple candies with sweet dried apricots, rich dark chocolate, and some salty cashew halves are the perfect dessert when you're looking for something simple to serve your guests. I often fill a decorative tin with these sweets and take it as a hostess gift in place of a bottle of wine. A perfect bite every time!

MAKES ABOUT 30 TO 35

½ cup semisweet chocolate chips

1 7- to 8-ounce package dried apricots, preferably organic

¼ cup cashew halves

1. Line a large baking sheet with parchment paper.

2. Warm the chocolate chips in a heatproof small bowl placed over a small saucepan of barely simmering water over low heat, stirring occasionally, just until the chips are almost but not completely melted. (The bottom of the bowl should not touch the water.) Remove from the heat and let stand, stirring occasionally, until the chocolate is completely melted and tepid, about 5 minutes.

3. Dip half of an apricot in the chocolate, dragging the bottom of the apricot on the edge of the bowl to remove excess chocolate. Place on the baking sheet and place a cashew half on it. Repeat with all of the apricots.

4. Refrigerate until the chocolate is set, about 15 minutes. Remove from the foil and serve chilled. To store, layer the candies between sheets of parchment or wax paper in a lidded container and refrigerate.

pineapple-chipotle popsicles

Discover your inner child with these very grown-up Popsicles! Pineapple and coconut milk are blended together with just a hint of chipotle powder to give just the slightest bit of heat. You need 8 4-ounce ice pop molds or 10 3-ounce wax-coated paper cups and ten wooden craft sticks.

MAKES 8 SERVINGS

2 cups fresh pineapple, peeled, cored, and coarsely chopped

¼ cup water

⅛ teaspoon chipotle powder

¾ cup canned unsweetened coconut milk

2 .035-ounce packets stevia or preferred sweetener

1. In a food processor, add the pineapple, water, chipotle powder, coconut milk and stevia and puree until completely smooth.

2. Spoon the pineapple mixture into 8 4-ounce ice pop molds or 10 3-ounce wax-coated paper cups. Freeze until frozen (if using paper cups, freeze until the pineapple mixture is semisolid; then insert a wooden craft stick into the center of each cup), at least 4 hours. Unmold and serve frozen.

Indulge!

mexican doughnuts (*sopapillas*)

When I say I'm going to indulge in dessert, I mean it. And that doesn't mean a slice of cake or a wedge of pie. An indulgent dessert for this chica can't be anything other than fried dough triangles drizzled with honey or sprinkled with cinnamon sugar.

MAKES 12 TO 18

2 cups all-purpose flour

2 teaspoons baking powder

1 tablespoon sugar

1 teaspoon salt

2 tablespoons vegetable shortening

¾ cup warm water, plus more as needed

peanut oil, for deep-frying

honey or cinnamon sugar, for serving

1. Sift the dry ingredients together into a large mixing bowl. Add the shortening and water; work them in with your fingertips to make a soft, pliable dough. If the dough feels too dry, add more water, 1 teaspoon at a time. Gather the dough into a ball and wrap in plastic wrap. Refrigerate for at least 1 hour until chilled and firm enough to roll. (The dough can be refrigerated up to 1 day before making the *sopapillas*.)

2. Unwrap the dough and cut it in half. Working with one half at a time, on a lightly floured surface, using a floured rolling pin, roll into a round about ¼ inch thick. Using a paring knife or pizza cutter, cut the dough into 6 to 8 triangles (just like a pizza).

3. Pour enough oil to come 2 inches up the side of a large heavy saucepan and heat to 375°F on a deep-frying thermometer. A few at a time, add the triangles to the oil and deep fry, flipping them over when they puff and rise to the surface of the oil, until golden brown, about 4 minutes. Using a wire skimmer or slotted spoon, transfer to paper towels or a brown paper bag to drain. Cool slightly. Serve hot with the honey or cinnamon sugar.

happy endings

acknowledgments

it has taken a dedicated team of loyal people to get me where I am today. You never see them, but they are the core and backbone of my business. They are the ones who have believed in me and have stuck by my side to help me accomplish my dreams.

You are all listed here; I have no words to thank you! I am grateful to all of you for your support, friendship, love and wisdom. Thank you from the bottom of my heart.

My family, who no matter what always jump on board and support, help and encourage me. Mom and Dad, you lead by example. You taught me what hard work is all about and what it is to have passion for what we do. Your love and nurturing have given me strength and courage. You inspire me. You both taught me the love of food. Mom, you worked with me since day one just because you believed in me. My sister Johanna, whose marketing skills, knowledge, love, and guidance helped me start and set up the Delicioso Brand dream in motion. My sister Annelies and brother-in-law, Jossy, for endless hours on my contracts and advising me, lending your home for photo shoots, etc. My kind, handsome nephews, whom I am so proud of: Franco, Diego, and Joshua. My aunt, Marlene, for encouraging my creative side. Maria Gomez for nurturing me early on.

my chica worldwide team

Delia Leon, you are Delicioso, my producer, my VP, my friend; you are my head, right and left hand, the heart and soul of this company. You are invaluable to me. You have stuck by me through thick and thin and have kept me together through all the dark moments. Your resilience, dedication, passion, and hard work are to be admired. You have taught me so much, especially what unwavering loyalty is. I could never have made it through the last seven years without you. Thank you for putting up with me and holding up the fort and gates and always protecting.

Andres Gomez, for your hard work, patience, and love. Aliza Stern, for making the Delicioso Univision transition so much easier and all the dedication, passion, and hard work.

Cathy Tomaiconza and Teresa Ramos, thanks for taking care of me and my home.

Thanks to my publicist and friend, Rebecca Brooks, and the chicas at the Brooks Group. Diana Baron of DBaron Media and Maria Ines for all of your amazing PR push. Lisa Shotland,

Rick Marroquin, and the rest of the CAA team, thanks for sticking by me and your hard work. Jamie Roberts, for your guidance. My literary agent, David Kuhn, at Kuhn Projects and his gang, for once again helping me make another book a reality.

my book team

Thanks to the team at Celebra/New American Library for believing in my vision.

To my collaborator, Harriet Bell, for not shying away from the craziest of deadlines. To Andrew Meade, friend and photographer extraordinaire, thank you for capturing my essence once again. Barbara Fritz, for the outstanding prop styling; to the best and most dynamic food-styling duo, Tami Hardeman and Abby Gaskins. To the Little River Studio team, Maureen Lutchejko and Susan Russo. Thank you all for helping me create a book I am very proud of.

in good company

Luis Balaguer/Latin World Entertainment, the first door I knocked on and keep knocking on! You have been my master and teacher. Julia Dangond, my very first producer ever. You are and always will be in my heart with great gratitude. Marla Acosta and Angela Fischer, for making sure I always look my best.

Univision Networks: César Conde, for believing in me. Margarita Black, Maria Lopez Alvarez, Luis Fernández, Vanessa Pombo, the *Despierta América* team, the *Delicioso with Ingrid Hoffmann* production team and crew, to my cohost and first-class lady, Maggie Jiménez, thank you. A very special thanks to Rick Allessandri, for believing in me and doing all you could to stand behind me.

my team at tfal

Thank you for the partnership in my first ever product line and for always shipping out pots and pans to wherever I am.

To the Coca-Cola family, I am proud to have the opportunity to experience what the Coke family is all about. You are the example of what corporate America should strive to be.

my friends

My nonpaid lawyers and friends, Steve Weinger and Andrew Ellenberg, for advising me always with love and dedication and just being there for me.

Jackie and Jonathan Chariff, for your endless love, support, and guidance.

Toni Almeida, trainer and spiritual mentor, for your friendship of twenty-three years; you are family. Cristine and Marc Tobin, Michelle and Scott Baena, Karla and Lizzy Dascal, Amy Zakarin, Lara Shriftman, Suzy Buckley, Lisi, Chabela, Hannah, Susan B, Paloma, Emma A, Alitza, Vivi F, Alan R, Martin K, Henry P, Kenneth N—your support, love, advice, and unconditional friendship have meant the world.

Paul Bacardi, my boyfriend and love, thanks for always cooking me Delicioso meals when I am tired. I love sharing food with you.

acknowledgments

index

index